teach yourself®

assertiveness

assertiveness

pat scudamore
and hilton catt

For over 60 years, more than 40 million people have learnt over 750 subjects the **teach yourself** way, with impressive results.

be where you want to be
with **teach yourself**

For UK order enquiries: please contact Bookpoint Ltd, 130 Milton Park, Abingdon, Oxon OX14 4SB. Telephone: +44 (0) 1235 827720. Fax: +44 (0) 1235 400454. Lines are open from 09.00–18.00, Monday to Saturday, with a 24-hour message answering service. You can aso order through our website www.teachyourself.co.uk

For USA order enquiries: please contact McGraw-Hill Customer Services, PO Box 545, Blacklick, OH 43004-0545, USA. Telephone: 1-800-722-4726. Fax: 1-614-755-5645.

For Canada order enquiries: please contact McGraw-Hill Ryerson Ltd, 300 Water St, Whitby, Ontario L1N 9B6, Canada. Telephone: 905 430 5000. Fax: 905 430 5020.

Long-renowned as the authoritative source for self-guided learning – with more than 30 million copies sold worldwide – the *Teach Yourself* series includes over 300 titles in the fields of languages, crafts, hobbies, business, computing and education.

British Library Cataloguing in Publication Data: a catalogue record for this title is available from The British Library.

Library of Congress Catalog Card Number: on file

First published in UK 2004 by Hodder Headline, 338 Euston Road, London NW1 3BH.

First published in US 2004 by Contemporary Books. a Division of The McGraw-Hill Companies, 1 Prudential Plaza, 130 East Randolph Street, Chicago, IL 60601, USA.

Typeset by Transet Limited, Coventry, England.
Printed in Great Britain for Hodder & Stoughton Educational, a division of Hodder Headline, 338 Euston Road, London NW1 3BH by Cox & Wyman Ltd., Reading, Berkshire.

Hodder Headline's policy is to use papers that are natural, renewable and recyclable products and made from wood grown in sustainable forests. The logging and manufacturing processes are expected to conform to the environmental regulations of the country of origin.

Impression number	10 9 8 7 6 5 4 3 2 1
Year	2010 2009 2008 2007 2006 2005 2004

contents

introduction

From time to time we all have concerns about whether we're being assertive enough. We see other people pushing themselves forward and getting noticed. We see how they don't hold back when it comes to expressing their opinions and ideas. We see our failings mirrored in their success and we wonder why we can't be more like them: more confident, more forceful, more adept at getting our own way.

Yet being more assertive has connotations with which not everyone is totally comfortable. Does it mean, for example, projecting a brash new image that could alienate our friends and perhaps open us to ridicule?

This Teach Yourself book is a practical, no-nonsense guide to the subject of assertiveness explaining:

- what it takes to become better at it;
- how, where and when to use it.

The book is divided into two parts:

Part One: Building Assertiveness deals with the issues we need to consider and the skills we need to acquire.

Part Two: Applying Assertiveness is about putting the techniques into practice in the real world in which we live and work.

As you work your way through the book you will come across a number of case studies that will enable you to draw on the experiences of others and learn from their successes and mistakes. At the end of each chapter you will find a section of questions and answers dealing with some of the problems that people come across, together with a summary.

What are the benefits to be gained from learning to be more assertive? These can be summarized as follows:

- greater confidence and self-esteem (feeling better about ourselves and the way we are);
- confidence to tap into our hidden talents and unleash our full potential;
- confidence to define and set out in pursuit of ambitions (greater control over our lives);
- the ability to stand up for ourselves and what we believe in;
- greater capacity to extend our beliefs and values to others and become more influential with family, friends, work colleagues alike;
- the success that comes from being more assertive in our relationships with others and in our business dealings, job applications, etc.

The best news of all perhaps is that this can be achieved without:

- a major overhaul of our personalities;
- anything else that could have the people we know fleeing for cover!

Test your assertiveness skills

Cast your eye over these ten questions and put a tick alongside the answer that most closely approximates the one you would give. See how you got on at the end.

Question 1

You've worked for a company for ten years where you've always been accustomed to knocking on the boss's door and waiting to be asked to come in. It has been suggested to you that this is wrong and a more assertive approach would be to forget the knocking and walk right in. Do you:

- A Stick to what you've always done and what you're comfortable with? ❑
- B Discuss the issue with your boss? ❑
- C Follow the suggestion? ❑
- D Knock, then go in, i.e. don't wait to be asked? ❑
- E Follow the suggestion but apologize later? ❑

Question 2

You arrive late for work one morning and have the bad luck to bump into your boss. As a result, your boss gives you a ticking off for bad timekeeping. In your opinion this isn't fair because others in the office have far worse timekeeping records than you. Do you:

- A Take issue with the boss? ❑
- B Write a letter of complaint to the Chief Executive? ❑

C Do nothing? ❑

D As C, except make an effort to ensure in future you arrive at work on time? ❑

E See what happens the next time the boss catches you coming in late? See if he gives you another ticking off and, if he does, respond by telling him to apply his disciplinary standards more consistently? ❑

Question 3

You got your present job thanks to an old friend putting in a good word for you. Now the friend is pestering you for business which would mean you stepping outside the rules in your firm for strict competitive tendering. Do you:

A Give your friend the business on the basis that one good turn deserves another? ❑

B Avoid the issue by taking no further phone calls from your friend? ❑

C Say no? ❑

D As C, except explain to your friend (a) the rules and (b) the dangers for you in failing to follow them? ❑

E Say you're no longer in the business of doing people favours? ❑

Question 4

You're not very happy with the salary you're being paid, and you've seen a number of your colleagues get rises by threatening to leave. Do you:

A Follow suit, presenting a case to your boss and threatening to hand your notice in if you don't get the figure you've named? ❑

B As A, but leave out the threat? ❑

C Say nothing? ❑

D Wait for the next salary review to come round? ❑

E Look for another job ❑

Question 5

You're asked to take on more responsibilities but you're told by the boss that there's no money in the budget to give an increase in your salary. Do you:

- A Refuse the additional responsibilities without the rise? ❑
- B Accept the additional responsibilities but under protest? ❑
- C Ask the boss for a commitment in writing that the rise will be paid to you in six months? ❑
- D Accept the offer as it stands? ❑
- E As D, then give the new responsibilities your best shot and put in for a rise as soon as you've proved yourself? ❑

Question 6

A subject of which you have limited knowledge comes up at a meeting and you're asked to given an opinion. You're worried that anything you say may lack substance and could open you up to challenges from the other people present (challenges you could find hard to defend). Do you:

- A Put the worries to one side and say what you think? ❑
- B Say you don't have an opinion? ❑
- C Come clean, say you don't know much about the subject and offer an opinion on that basis? ❑
- D Say you agree with the last speaker? ❑
- E Try and bluff everyone into thinking you know more than you do? ❑

Question 7

You've made a terrible blunder with a price you've quoted to a customer and, as a result, your company stands to lose a significant amount of money. Do you:

- A Shrug it off (say everyone makes mistakes)? ❑
- B Find someone else to blame? ❑
- C Offer to resign? ❑
- D Admit your mistake and say you're sorry? ❑
- E Say nothing? ❑

Question 8

After putting up the most convincing case you can assemble, a major decision goes against you (your company decides to outsource its human resources management function to a firm of consultants). You feel that in reaching this decision your company failed to take into account a number of important factors and, as a consequence, you are convinced that you and other senior managers could be plunged into insurmountable difficulties when dealing with HR issues in future. Do you:

- **A** Resign in protest? ❑
- **B** Put your disagreement with the decision into writing? ❑
- **C** Put the matter behind you and get on with life? ❑
- **D** Wait for the problems to start and, when they do, tell your company you told them so? ❑
- **E** Prove your point by making the decision unworkable e.g. by making life difficult for the consultants? ❑

Question 9

You seem to get passed by every time an opportunity for promotion comes up. Others get the chances but not you. Do you:

- **A** Put this down to their ability to be more pushy? ❑
- **B** Ask yourself if you've made your ambitions known sufficiently? ❑
- **C** Blame your bosses for failing to notice you? ❑
- **D** Look for another job? ❑
- **E** Complain? ❑

Question 10

After working very satisfactorily for a company for a number of years, you get a new boss who is highly critical of everything you do to the point that you start to doubt your own competence. Do you:

- **A** See if you can get a transfer elsewhere in the company, i.e. work for someone else? ❑
- **B** Put up with the criticism? ❑
- **C** Look for another job? ❑
- **D** Take issue with your new boss and say you won't put up with any more criticism? ❑
- **E** Make an official complaint to the Chief Executive? ❑

How did you get on?

The answers we are looking for are as follows:

Question 1	A
Question 2	D
Question 3	D
Question 4	B
Question 5	E
Question 6	C
Question 7	D
Question 8	C
Question 9	B
Question 10	A or C

Why? Read the book and find out.

part one

building assertiveness

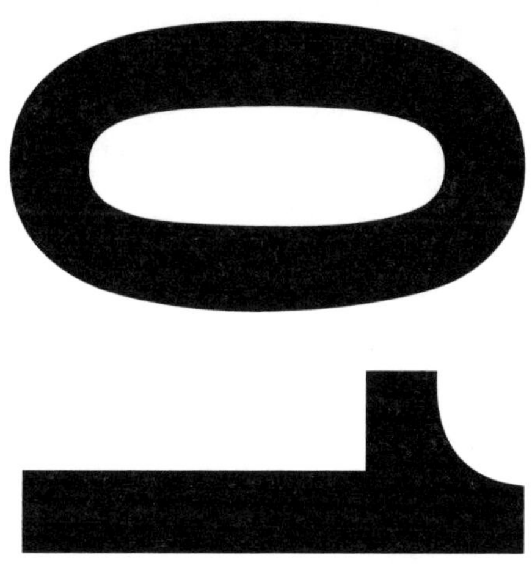

1 the power of you

In this chapter you will learn:

- how to identify what's in the way of you becoming more assertive
- how to get rid of negative influences
- how to take control of your life
- how to improve your image

You and what you stand for

Assertiveness starts with feeling good about:

- you;
- what you stand for.

You will find it difficult to be assertive if you have a low opinion of yourself or if you don't attach much importance to your views and ideas. How do you know if you come into this category? Cast your eyes down the following checklist and be honest with yourself. The more questions you answer 'yes' to, the more likely it is that your first step in becoming more assertive will be to take a long hard look at your self-esteem.

Checklist: How high is your self-esteem?

- Do you hold back in conversations because it worries you that anything you say either won't be very interesting or could sound foolish?
- Do you think most people are more switched on and/or cleverer than you?
- Do you admire people who are good at asserting themselves? Do you wish you could be more like them?
- Do you think that other people are better than you when it comes to winning arguments?
- Do you feel you let yourself down by not always standing up for what you believe to be right?
- Do you prefer to listen to what other people have got to say rather than express your own ideas?
- Do you allow your opinions to be steam-rollered by people who you view as having more forceful personalities than you?
- Do you feel underpaid and/or undervalued yet there's nothing you can do about it?

What to do about low self-esteem

Low self-esteem is at the root of most difficulties people have with becoming more assertive. They don't have enough confidence in themselves, they're uncertain about their beliefs and values and, not surprisingly, they find it hard to convince others that:

- they know what they're talking about;
- what they're saying is right.

But what can be done to improve low self-esteem? How can we overcome it?

Identifying negative influences

This is your first stopping-off point in:

- seeking to eliminate anything that could be getting in the way of raising the level of your self-esteem;
- empowering you in the quest to become more assertive.

The question is this: is there any influence in your life that is undermining you and the way you feel about yourself? You are the only one in a position to answer this question, of course, but just to give you some clues on the directions you should be looking in, let's go to the first of our case studies. This is the story of Jenny. Jenny's self-esteem is being undermined by someone who occupies a very influential position in her life. Let's see how it affects her:

Case study 1: Jenny

Jenny works as a Production Assistant in a plant which manufactures fibres for the textile industry. Jenny is 26 and she has been in this position for the last three and a half years. It is the only job she has ever had.

Jenny's boss is Andy, the Production Manager, and here she has a problem. Nothing she does for Andy ever seems to be right. Every time she makes a decision, Andy can usually find some reason for pulling her up and finding fault in it. Any ideas she puts forward at meetings, Andy immediately tears them to pieces, to the point where she now keeps her ideas to herself. As to praise, no words of encouragement or thanks for a job well done have ever passed Andy's lips.

Though it strikes Jenny that many of Andy's criticisms are pedantic, she is finding lately that she is starting to question her own abilities. At one time she had high hopes for herself in terms of what she could achieve in a business career, but now she is not so sure.

What we see here is someone whose self-esteem is being undermined by an over-critical and unsupportive boss. What we don't know is:

- whether the criticism is deserved;
- whether Andy has got a higher opinion of Jenny than she thinks and that he's just bad at communicating his true feelings;
- whether he's trying to put her down because, for example, he's insecure, and feels threatened by a bright young member of staff in his department (someone who could step into his shoes one day).

Yet in many ways, the game Andy is playing hardly matters. All that is important for Jenny is the effect his negative influence is having on her self-esteem. She is already having doubts about herself. She is frightened about putting forward her ideas and opinions in meetings. She is in fact on a downward spiral which, as time goes on, will get worse and worse. At some stage in the future she will reach a point where she is going to find herself believing in what she sees as her own inadequacies – that is unless she can find some way of disengaging from the negative conditioning forces that are working on her.

Key point

If you are concerned about your self-esteem, identifying any negative forces that may be at work on you is an important first step. If by default you are allowing people to condition you into doubting your own worth, then you need to do something about it. If you let this situation go on, it will:

- affect the quality of your life;
- inhibit you in the forming of your ambitions;
- prevent you from exercising your true potential;
- cause you to underachieve.

Ridding yourself of negative influences

Now comes the hard part. Once you've identified the people in your life who are stopping you feeling good about yourself and causing you to have doubts about your abilities, how do you go about removing yourself from them?

The real Jenny in our case study finally decided that, as far as Andy was concerned, enough was enough. She went out and found another job and, since then, her career has never looked back. What's so hard about this, you may be asking? Surely anyone with a boss like Andy would decide to move on sooner or later?

The hard part is that, because your low self-esteem clogs up your vision, what to most of us may seem like the logical thing to do won't be viewed in the same way by someone harbouring major doubts themselves. Because they have no belief in their own judgement, they will find it hard to be firm and decisive. Yet firm and decisive is what they need to be. So full marks to Jenny for putting herself first. Full marks to her for seeing the problem and dealing with it.

Keeping your distance from people who undermine you

Severing the connections with bosses and work colleagues who are undermining your self-esteem may simply be a matter of changing jobs, but what if the person who is having a negative influence on you is a friend or a member of your family? What if you don't have the option of making a clean break and never seeing them again? Take the example of Matt. Matt has known Gemma for most of his life. They went to the same school together, their families are friends and they live in the same neighbourhood. Gemma, however, is bossy, outspoken and given to lecturing Matt on what she tells him are his shortcomings. Matt, for his part, has always taken Gemma's comments to heart but, now he's a little older, he realizes that Gemma's influence is one of the reasons why he has little confidence in himself. With Gemma such a close member of his circle, telling her to stay out of his life is probably not an option that Matt would want to pursue. What he can do, however, is keep his distance from her by having as little to do with her as possible. In this way he will:

- acknowledge the undermining effect she is having;
- prevent it from happening any more.

Warning

Differentiate between people who are undermining you and those who are telling you home truths for your own good. Shutting out the latter would clearly be a big mistake. How do you spot the difference? People who undermine you do so by being negative, whereas those who are trying to help you will always been keen to point out ways forward.

Disengage from bad job situations

This is a word in the ear of those of you who may feel you are undervalued or underpaid. Going on year after year without proper recognition of your talents or of the input you make has an insidious and sapping effect on your self-esteem. The short message here is don't let it happen, because you will find yourself descending to a low from which you will find it hard to get back. Disengage from bad job situations. Employ your talents where they will be recognized. Properly.

The importance of you

To sum up, what we have done so far is to get you to identify and deal with any influences that may be eroding your self-esteem. This, in a way, is clearing the ground for the next part of the process, which is getting you to feel good about yourself so you're able to mean it when you say:

- I'm important;
- What I think is important too.

Give yourself a treat

This may sound trivial but, as part of attaching proper importance to yourself, you've got to see yourself as someone worth spending money on. People with low self-esteem don't spend money on themselves for the simple reason they don't think they're worth it. So, as a symbolic gesture of making a clean break with the past, identify something you would really like and, go on, splash out and have it. Most importantly, don't feel guilty about being extravagant. Instead, see the new suit, the weekend in the luxury hotel, the meal in the Michelin-starred restaurant as making an important statement. You're not going to be down-trodden any more. The future is going to be different.

Key point
If you don't respect yourself, don't expect respect from anyone else.

Your image

The word 'image' has unfortunate connotations, so let's say straight away it's not our intention to turn you into a fashion icon. Rather we want you to see that, to exercise assertiveness successfully, people have got to have confidence in you and this won't happen if you don't look the part. What you need to do therefore is pay attention to items such as your clothes and personal grooming. The aim here is to have you looking your best every day, not just when you've got an important meeting to go to or an interview to attend. Leave the dressing down to others.

Notepad
Presenting a good image and giving your best to every day is a subject we will be returning to later in this chapter (see p. 20, The Lifelong Interview).

How to lift your image

Are there any tips we can give you on what you can do to give your image a lift?

- Go through your wardrobe and throw out anything that's faded, lost its shape or gone out of fashion. This will take away the temptation to wear any such items – for example, on days when you feel dispirited or can't be bothered.
- Select clothes that go with your lifestyle. For example, if you work in an office, you will need clothes that are smart, comfortable and will stay looking good all day.
- Try to build up a good basic wardrobe of clothes and accessories you can mix and match. This will enable you to make daily changes to your appearance without it costing you a fortune.
- Spread the cost of your wardrobe by replacing a certain number of items every year. A planned approach on these lines will also help you to take full advantage of opportunities, such as bargain shopping breaks.

- Remember that, whilst there's nothing wrong with a bargain, cheap isn't always good.
- Put your clothes on a regular cleaning cycle. Make it a rule never to wear anything that looks grubby or could have picked up either kitchen or tobacco smells.
- Always go to a good hair stylist. The extra money it costs is well worth it.
- Pay attention to personal cleanliness. Hands and fingernails are especially important.
- Remember to clean your shoes.

Notepad

One of the spin-offs from smartening up your image is that you will immediately feel better. The knock-on effect is that your levels of self-esteem will automatically go up. In terms of improving your capacity to be more assertive, the benefits are huge.

Taking control of your life

An important part of feeling good about yourself is to be in control of your life. A life that's out of control will:

- sap at your self-esteem and undermine your confidence
- distract you from what you really want to be doing in your life.

The golden rule as far as managing your life is concerned is to keep it as simple as you possibly can, because the less threads you have running through it, the easier it will be to manage. By keeping it simple you can then avoid becoming bogged down by complications, and keep your focus on the things that are important to you.

Set your agenda

Decide what you want out of life – in other words have some aims which, for convenience sake, you can divide into:

- **Small aims**, such as saving up enough money to buy a better car, or learning to use some new IT software.
- **Big aims**, such as being Chief Executive of your firm by the time you're 40, or going off to live and work overseas within the next five years.

With these aims in place, you can decide how you're going to work towards them (your agenda). You will feel you have a purpose and your self-esteem will benefit from the importance you are attaching to your ideas. We will look more fully at the importance of defining your aims in Chapter 6.

Keep in control of your finances

Money troubles can be undermining and you won't get far with unleashing the power of you if you are constantly locked in a struggle to pay the bills On the other hand, having the cash available to back up your grand plans is very empowering and will do wonders for your self-confidence.

What are the secrets of keeping your finances under control?

1 Again, keep it simple. Finances that are complicated take a lot more managing and, with other pressures on your time, there's always the chance of an oversight when your eye isn't one hundred per cent on the ball.
2 Try as far as you can to stay out of debt. Why? For the simple reason that if you're in debt you're placing yourself in the hands of banks, finance companies and the like. In other words, they're in control and you aren't.
3 Manage your finances, by which we mean do your sums every month including projections on your incomings and outgoings. Don't get caught out by quirks in cashflow.
4 Perhaps most importantly, try to make your finances as *flexible* as possible, by which we mean try to avoid too many large fixed overheads such as large fixed rate mortgages. In today's world, where earnings fluctuate year on year and nothing is certain it is better by far to have outgoings that you can adjust upwards or downwards depending on the circumstances. Again, it puts you more in control and you're not forced along paths because paying the bills dictates that you don't have a choice.
5 Get into the savings habit. Having a war chest you can dip into gives you a great feeling of security. It serves as yet another confidence booster.

Notepad

In the question and answers at the end of this chapter we offer advice to someone who is in a substantial amount of debt (see p. 25, 'My finances are a mess'.)

The Lifelong Interview

So far we've been putting the pieces in place that will serve as the forerunner to unleashing the power of you, the first step on the path to greater assertiveness. We have:

- encouraged you to be firm and decisive when it comes to dealing with people who undermine you – either to sever the connections with them altogether or, if this proves too difficult, to keep them at an arm's length and have as little to do with them as possible;
- sought to give a boost to your self-esteem by getting you to attach proper importance to yourself and what you stand for;
- encouraged you to take control of your life so it's you who is in the driving seat, you who determines the direction you go in, and you who is in control of your money.

What we want to look at next is how you need to project yourself if you want assertiveness to work for you – the type of image you should be trying to put across and how to go about acquiring it.

Why image is important

We have touched on image already in the context of how our personal appearance impacts on others, and how it serves as a decisive factor in determining whether they are going to have confidence in us or not (whether our assertiveness will or won't work on them).

Yet the point about image stretches much further and, to understand the full implications, it may be useful to look at another case study. This is the story of Winston and Zena, two senior managers in a food processing and packaging company who are seeking to influence their boss's thinking on a key decision.

Case study 2: Winston and Zena

AAA Foods are looking to make an important appointment – someone to head up a new venture into which the parent company will be investing a substantial sum of money over the next three years.

There are two contenders for the job:

- Kuldip, who is a bright, up-and-coming member of the engineering team and the protégé of Winston, the Operations Manager;

- Colin, a high-flying account executive who works for Zena, the Head of Sales.

It will be up to Mike, the Managing Director, to decide who gets the new job and, with the need to appoint someone becoming pressing, he calls Winston and Zena to a meeting to ask their opinion. With both of them he realizes they will be gunning for their own man. The opportunity to extend their influence over the way the new venture is run won't have escaped either of them.

Predictably Winston puts up a very convincing case for Kuldip. He points to the desirability of having someone with a technical background in charge of the new venture because of the high levels of investment in plant and machinery. He is full of praise for Kuldip's character and management skills.

When it comes to Zena's turn, she is equally convincing in the argument she puts forward for Colin. The new venture needs someone who can go out and find business with good margins and, on that criterion alone, it will either succeed or fail. On this score, Colin is the ideal man. What's more he's steady and reliable and ready for promotion. What better candidate could there be?

Over the next few days Mike reflects on what Winston and Zena had to say. The way he sees it is as follows. The new venture is something he personally fought for so, in finding the right person to run it, he needs first and foremost someone with a safe pair of hands who can carry the project through. With Kuldip and Colin, it is true that two of his senior managers have vouched for their characters but, in Winston's case, Mike is not sure about the quality of his judgement. Winston's career with the company stretches back 15 years and it has been chequered to say the least. Indeed, as recently as 18 months ago, Mike had to take Winston to task about his behaviour at a company function (behaviour that resulted from Winston having too much to drink).

Mike has no such qualms about Zena. She is relatively new to the company having joined from a competitor just over two years ago. She has always conducted herself very professionally and he feels he can trust her. On that basis he decides to offer the job to Colin. He is sure that is nothing wrong with Kuldip but he can't afford to take the chance.

The points to pick out from this case study are as follows:

- Both Winston and Zena appear to have been equally assertive.
- Winston's assertiveness didn't work on Mike because of what Mike knew about him.
- A similar problem didn't arise for Zena because (a) Mike knew less about her and (b) what he did know was good.

Giving your best to every day

The case study illustrates how your ability to make the best out of being assertive links directly to the quality of the image you project. The assertiveness worked for Zena because her image was good. On the contrary, it failed to work for Winston because his image had a few dents and cracks in it.

The lesson? Simply this: you need to be very mindful of the image you project as you go about your day-to-day business because this will have a direct bearing on how successful you are going to be when it comes to getting others to accept your ideas and opinions.

Key point

The concept of the *Lifelong Interview* is to make a comparison between the image you project when you go for a interview for a job you would really like to get and the one you put across every day. In the case of the former, you will take the trouble to dress smartly. You will make sure you are on your best behaviour. You will be careful about anything you say and, if there are any grey areas in your past history, you will do your utmost to conceal them. Not so, however, with the rather less well-managed image you project to those who come into contact with you daily. You may not always pay full attention to your appearance. You are not so guarded in your conversations. You may even be like Winston and let your hair down occasionally so some less endearing aspect of your personality accidentally slips out. The problem here, of course, is that we're talking about projecting an image day in, day out, rather than for the duration of the relatively short period of time it takes to have an interview for a job. Harder? Yes of course it is. The focus and consistency called for are not easy to achieve.

How to project the right image

We have already looked at how your appearance (your choice of clothes and your personal grooming) impacts on your ability to make assertiveness work for you. But what else? In what other ways do you need to be mindful of the image you project as you go about your day-to-day business? The following is a list of examples:

The Lifelong Interview in practice: examples

- You can't afford to have 'off' days.
- Don't get drawn into office gossip and tittle-tattle.
- Don't run down your bosses and/or colleagues behind their backs.
- Don't blame others for your mistakes – if it's you that's at fault then own up to it.
- Give some of the gloss you save up for interviews to every day.

Keep your flaws to yourself

Most of us have flaws, but whether we broadcast them or not is a matter for us to choose. In Winston's case he misbehaved himself at a company function (a very visible occasion) and he paid the price in terms of losing Mike's confidence in his judgement. How much better it would have been for Winston if he'd managed to indulge his liking for a drink or two away from his workplace (somewhere where it didn't matter).

Questions and answers

The negative influence is my partner

Q *For the last two years I've been combining studying for a degree with working full time and trying to run a home. With the degree, I hope to realize a long-cherished ambition to train for a career in veterinary work. My problem, however, is my partner. He keeps telling me I'm wasting my time and that I should stick to doing something that's more within my capabilities. As you can imagine, comments such as these are having an undermining effect on my self-esteem. However, as I live with my partner and see him every day, the option of keeping him at a distance is not one that is open to me. Any suggestions?*

A It sounds like everything else is fine in your relationship with your partner except for his sniping at your abilities and ambitions. Could it be that your partner sees your studies as intrusive in terms of the time you should be spending together? In which case it may be worth taking some time out with the aim of:

- communicating to him how unfair he's being;
- pointing out the benefits to him if you're successful in getting into your new career (more money presumably; greater scope with what you can afford to do in the time you spend together);
- telling him that, if he carries on sniping at you, it will put a rift between you (this is to show you're serious);
- getting him to change his ways and become more supportive.

Why is this worth trying? An emotional bust-up with someone who is close to you won't do you much good when you're trying to do the work-life-study balancing act, and if you carry on as you are, an emotional bust-up sounds very much on the cards. Conversely, an encouraging and supportive partner will be an enormous asset to you as you seek to realize your ambitions.

Keeping it simple is not possible for me

Q *I'm a single mum and, although I'm determined to make the best of my situation, the juggling act of looking after two children, holding down a job and running a home makes it difficult for me to see how I can keep my life simple. Is this really for me?*

A Keeping it simple is part of keeping control of your life and, yes, in your case, we can see that this must be difficult. What might help is to try as far as possible to put your life into compartments (e.g. work, home, family) and to apply the simplicity rules within those compartments. It may not be perfect, but if it helps to instil some sense of order it will at least be progress towards taking away the kind of complications that could become a distraction to you.

My finances are a mess

Q *I agree entirely with all you have to say about money troubles and the undermining effect they have on self-esteem. My problem, however, is that I am there already. Following the collapse of my business six months ago and the subsequent break-up of my marriage, I'm literally up to my ears in bills and I know sooner or later I will have to face up to court actions. What I am considering is taking on a loan to get myself straight, but in many ways this goes against the grain. What do you think? The good news is I'm back in steady, well-paid employment.*

A There is a big distinction between taking on a loan to get your life back in order and using it to fund over-spending. With the latter you need to address the real problem first, whereas with the former a loan will enable you to clear the decks, get some of your self-esteem back and put you on the road to recovery. With a steady income coming in you can hopefully look forward to repaying the loan quickly, but make this a priority because to be out of debt will give yet a further boost to your self-esteem.

My Lifelong Interview is blown

Q *I think I may have made the same mistakes as Winston in your case study 2. I've not got a very good track record with my company, and over the years I've had numerous warnings about failing to meet targets and not putting in sufficient effort. Is this a case of 'forget it' as far as the exercise of assertiveness is concerned? If so, would it be best for me to find another job where I can make a fresh start?*

A The decision to leave a company is not one to be taken lightly, particularly if you have been there a number of years. What's more, there are many factors to be taken into account when determining whether it's the right time to make a job move or not. Bear in mind as well that it's never too late to turn over a new leaf, although you may have to accept that your bosses will want to see a sustained performance from you over a period of time before reappraising their assessment of you.

Summary

In Chapter 1, we have been looking at what it takes to unleash the power of you – the power of you being one of the four foundation stones on which assertiveness is built. We started by trying to identify any negative influences that may be working on you in the shape of people who – whether they do it consciously or not – undermine your self-esteem either by their words, or by their deeds, or both. We saw in case study 1 (Jenny) the damage this undermining can do and how important it is to put a stop to it.

We next turned to examining ways of giving your self-confidence a boost by getting you to see yourself and what you stand for as important and not to be compromised in any way. We saw how it helps in this respect to have your life under control so you are not distracted by unnecessary complications.

Finally in this chapter, we looked at the image you need to project if you want assertiveness to work for you. We saw how people need to have confidence in you and how you have to win that confidence by paying attention to the way you conduct yourself (the lifelong interview).

02 the power of knowledge

In this chapter you will learn:

- how to add to your capacity to be more assertive by adding to your range of skills, knowledge and experience
- what silent bargaining power means
- how to exercise leverage

Adding value to yourself

In the last chapter we saw how, to make assertiveness work for you, people need to have confidence in:

- you;
- your ideas and opinions.

We dealt with the first of these points under the heading of The Lifelong Interview. Now let us turn our attention to the second. What does it take to make people listen to and value what you're saying? What makes them sit up and take note? Again, a case study will help. This is the story of Melissa, a bright young graduate with lots of ideas that she is keen to share with everyone.

Case study 3: Melissa

Melissa is 22 and fresh out of university with a first class honours degree in Business Administration. Her ambition is to get into marketing and she has successfully landed a job in the marketing department of one the major players in the mobile telecommunications industry.

During her induction period, Melissa starts to acquire the reputation of being a know-it-all. She expresses her opinions freely and the people who are responsible for showing her the ropes find she has a tendency not to listen. However, worse is to come.

Two months into her new job, Melissa is attached to a project team. At the end of her first week of working on the team she is asked to attend a meeting at which two senior colleagues are present, along with the Marketing Manager. Seeing this as an opportunity to impress everybody, Melissa decides to ignore the advice of her team leader to stay in the background. Instead, she practically takes over the meeting and uses it as a platform for her own ideas. The fact that most of these ideas are half-baked and unworkable is completely lost on Melissa. She continues to hammer home her arguments until finally the Marketing Manager excuses himself saying he has another meeting to go to.

Over the next few days, Melissa and her over-assertiveness is the talk of the office. The general opinion is that someone ought to have a word in her ear.

Here we have someone who has no problems with being assertive, but who has nothing to back it up in terms of job knowledge and experience. As a result, she makes herself into an object of ridicule, and for this reason her assertiveness hasn't worked.

Hopefully someone will have a word in Melissa's ear and she will listen to the advice she is given.

Warning

Don't try to be assertive if:

- you're not sure of your facts;
- the subject under discussion is outside the range of your skills, knowledge and experience.

If you do you could end up like Melissa, i.e. looking foolish and no further forward in the task of convincing people that your opinions and ideas should be taken seriously.

Identifying shortcomings in your skills, knowledge and experience

Since you need to know *what* you're talking about before you try to be assertive, you need to identify any areas where there are gaps in your skills, knowledge and experience, and see what you can do to fill those gaps. In Melissa's case what she clearly needs to do is to put her assertiveness on hold until she has got some job experience under her belt. No one is questioning the fact that she is bright and, properly channelled, she will probably go on to be a great asset to her employer and do well for herself in years to come.

Applying selectivity

This is simply a reminder that no one is an expert in everything. In other words, you need to judge when a subject falls within the range of your skills, knowledge and experience and when it doesn't. In the first case you can feel free to be assertive, whereas in the second, it may be best to keep quiet and listen to what everyone else is saying. Don't be afraid to say, 'Sorry I don't know anything about this.' This will give you greater credibility when subjects come up on which you really do have something important to offer.

Notepad

Where (and where not) to use assertiveness is a subject we will be returning to in more detail in Chapter 4.

Key point

In today's world, people are valued by:

- what they can do;
- how much they know.

This is why you must always seek to extend the range of your skills, knowledge and experience. See life as a continuous learning process. Take advantage of any opportunities that are offered to you.

Silent bargaining power

This is where we start to draw together some of the lessons covered so far in this book. We have seen how there is a direct link between getting assertiveness to work for you and how other people see you in terms of:

- the image you project;
- what you know and what you can do (your skills, knowledge and experience).

We have expressed this link in terms of value and we have noted how you can add to your value by:

- improving your image;
- adding to the range of your skills, knowledge and experience.

Put another way, people will attach importance to you and what you're saying if they value you. Conversely, they will take no notice of you if they feel you and your opinions are of little consequence – and this is irrespective of how assertive you are.

Your clout with other people

In this way, your value equates to the clout you carry with people, and this clout is, in turn, your *silent bargaining power*. Why 'silent'? For the simple reason that you don't spend your time going round reminding your circle of family, friends, work colleagues, bosses, business contacts, etc. that you're important and every word that comes out of your mouth is important too. They need to know without being told. Indeed, if you did resort to blowing your own trumpet too much, these same people would probably start to wonder why you were behaving in this way.

How to measure your silent bargaining power

How much clout do you carry with key figures in your life? Is there any way of measuring it?

A useful test to apply is to ask yourself how the people in question would react if you suddenly walked out on them. Would they miss you? Or would they be clapping their hands with glee at seeing the back of you? In the question and answers section at the end of Chapter 1, we gave advice to someone with a very critical and unsupportive partner (see p. 23, 'The negative influence is my partner'). In this instance, it is interesting to speculate on how the partner concerned would react if our questioner decided to walk out on him. Would it be good riddance or would the partner have cause for regret? In the latter case it would clearly be in the partner's interests to start listening and taking note.

Warning

Not for one minute are we suggesting that you should make threats to take yourself off. This is *silent* bargaining power, remember, and the force is contained in the thoughts that pass through the other person's head, not in the words that come out of your mouth. As to threats, you should never make them unless you are prepared to carry them out. Otherwise the only option you leave yourself with is to back down, thus negating straightaway any benefits gained from your assertiveness.

Leverage

Bringing silent bargaining power to bear is known as leverage, and the way in which it works is illustrated in our next case study, the tale of Lucas.

Case study 4: Lucas

Lucas works as a buyer for a small company of electrical distributors. He is 34 and he has been in this position for the last seven years.

Lucas has always taken a keen interest in IT. Computers are his hobby and he has done a number of courses on programming, mostly in his own time.

As the use of computerized systems spreads in the company, Lucas becomes involved firstly in the purchasing of hardware and software and then in various upgradings that take place. He designs the company's website which receives a great deal of favourable comment from both suppliers and customers alike. He acts as the company's IT trouble-shooter and, over the years, people have found it easier to ask Lucas to take a look at the problem than to try and sort it out for themselves. Lucas is always obliging. He never says 'sorry' or 'too busy'. He is always there when help is needed.

In recent months, Lucas has become concerned about his pay. This has been partly brought on by the company's decision to put a freeze on salaries and partly because he feels he is falling behind the market rate for buyers with his experience. One evening after work he mentions these concerns to Annette, the company's Administration Manager, who is his immediate boss. Annette listens carefully to everything he has to say, but makes no comment other than she'll think about it and get back to him. Annette, for her part, realizes that, if there are going to be any exceptions to the freeze on salaries, she will have to get the agreement of David, the Managing Director. In other words, saying 'yes' to Lucas is outside her remit.

At first David is hostile to the idea of giving Lucas a salary increase. He points to the fact that no one is happy with the freeze on their pay and, if it got out that an exception had been made for Lucas, he would have everyone knocking at his door. Annette, however, is quick to point out that the company would be the loser if Lucas chose to get the level of salary he wanted by taking his talents elsewhere. It would not just be a case of replacing a buyer, they would also have to find some way of providing IT cover and this could prove to be expensive. Certainly there is no one else on the staff with Lucas's knowledge, no one else who would either be willing or able to take on Lucas's IT role.

The key points to pick out from this case study are as follows:

- Lucas has made a great job of his Lifelong Interview.
- By being helpful and obliging he has succeeded in projecting a good image.
- He has added to his value by adding to his range of skills, knowledge and experience (including going on courses in his own time).
- As a consequence of the first two points here, he has amassed a quite formidable store of silent bargaining power.
- The leverage has worked on Annette. She realizes that saying 'no' to Lucas could mean him leaving. She realizes the damage this would inflict on the company, and through Annette this leverage is passed on to David.
- Lucas's assertion that he deserves better pay is taken seriously by his two bosses. Hopefully it will bring about the outcome he wants – a rise.

Cornering areas of expertise

What is also interesting to note in this case study is that, intentionally or not, Lucas has worked a very clever trick. He has effectively *cornered* the IT expertise in his company, and he has done this by being willing and helpful so that other members of staff have come to rely on him. This has added greatly to his silent bargaining power and to his capacity to make assertiveness work. At the same time it illustrates how people who don't put barriers around themselves in terms of what they're prepared to do can profit enormously.

Knowledge is power

What the case study also illustrates is that, if you know your stuff, people will automatically come to you for information and guidance. As a result, you may find you have little need for assertiveness because your ideas and opinions will be accepted irrespective of the way you put them over.

Improve your general knowledge

Your capacity to be assertive will be enhanced if you can demonstrate to everyone that you have got a good general knowledge – knowledge that extends outside the field of knowledge you need to do your job. People who have a wide appreciation of what's going on in the world and can offer opinions on a range of subjects are not just interesting to talk to, they also command a respect which adds further to the feeling of confidence in what they say.

How do you go about improving your general knowledge? Firstly, there are no short cuts and, to some readers, it could mean a reassessment of their lifestyles. Here are a few tips:

- Try to make a point of reading a good broadsheet newspaper every day. Read it from cover to cover including, for example, the arts sections and the book reviews even though they may not directly interest you.
- Keep a good book on the go, for bedtime reading or to pass the time on journeys. Try to mix fiction with non-fiction. With the latter try to use your choice of non-fiction reading to extend your general knowledge into areas where it may currently be weak. For example, if your knowledge of European History since the Second World War is hazy then it may be worth casting your eye along the appropriate shelves in the bookshop.
- Try to include news and current affairs programmes in your television watching and radio listening. Make a point of catching documentaries that sound interesting.
- Do something different, for example break out of your normal social routines and attempt something that will stretch you. Have you considered learning a foreign language at an evening class at the local college?

Warning

Don't expect to see immediate results from following the above advice. The improvement to your general knowledge and, as a consequence, your standing with others will only come over a period of time. The watchwords are:

- keep at it;
- be patient.

Questions and answers

Who pays?

Q *No one is disputing that knowledge is a fine thing but, in the case of job knowledge, who pays for the training? I ask because my company is notoriously tight-fisted when it comes to footing the bill to let people go on courses. As a result, many of us feel at a disadvantage when we have to go to meetings to discuss business with clients.*

A Your company has clearly got problems, but whether this has been brought about by financial constraints or antiquated attitudes is hard to tell from your question. Have you and your colleagues tried putting a case for training to your bosses? Collectively you must have sufficient silent bargaining power to be able to exercise considerable leverage on them. If not, it may be worth giving it a go, but read the rest of this book first. However, there is a more fundamental point at issue here. In today's world you can no longer rely on employers to meet your training needs – some will, some won't. Remember, this is your career and looking after the training and development plan is up to you. So, yes, it may mean you have to keep your job knowledge up to specification by studying in your own time and footing the bills yourself, but don't view this as unfair because it won't help you. You may find one of our other books in the Teach Yourself series interesting reading (*Teach Yourself Managing Your Own Career*). This goes into the question you've raised in much more detail.

No time to improve my general knowledge

Q *I would love to do something about my general knowledge, but frankly there aren't enough hours in the day for me to fit in the kind of self-improvement activities you suggest. Any advice for me?*

A Work–life balance is a subject that affects us all, so we fully understand the difficulties. However, what's at stake here is your capacity to become better at influencing others and gaining a greater level of acceptance for your opinions and ideas. In short you need to make absolutely sure that your life is as tightly packed as you say it is. An interesting exercise to carry out is to look at what you do with your time over the space of, say, a week. Are you duplicating? Is there anything you can cut out? Could other people in your life help you to make a bit of space for yourself?

Cornering knowledge

Q *Surely cornering knowledge goes completely against the philosophy of knowledge-based organizations where experience and know-how is shared with colleagues. Are you seriously suggesting that keeping our knowledge to ourselves is something we should be striving to do?*

A Our comments about knowledge cornering were not intended as a value judgement but rather as an observation on how people can (and do) amass quite formidable stocks of silent bargaining power which they can then use to their advantage. Whether it's good or not rather depends on where you're sitting. Certainly as far as employers are concerned it can mean some individuals will have them well and truly over a barrel.

Summary

Anyone can be assertive, but it won't do you much good if the person on the receiving end of your assertiveness has little or no confidence in the substance of what you are saying. This will happen if the other person knows you are not qualified and/or experienced enough to be voicing opinions on a certain subject.

In Chapter 2, we have seen that, to get the most out of assertiveness, there is no substitute for knowing your stuff. Here we've encouraged you to see your range of skills, knowledge and experience as your value in the eyes of others. This is what makes them attach importance to what you are saying. In examining silent bargaining power and the exercise of leverage, we've seen what it takes to make people sit up and take notice of you. Sometimes you may need to be assertive and sometimes you won't. The tactics you use to get over your arguments will depend on the circumstances and we will be looking at this further in Chapter 4.

Finally, never view skills, knowledge and experience as static, but instead as personal assets that you can acquire and go on acquiring. The benefit to you will be to boost your capacity to use assertiveness successfully.

Key point

To be assertive you also need to be right.

the power of communication

In this chapter you will learn:

- how to make oral communication work
- when to put it into writing
- why it's important to take account of people

Why communication skills are important

In this chapter we're going to look at the third of the four foundation stones to the successful use of assertiveness: your ability to put over your views and opinions to others in a way that they are going to find convincing. Again, let's begin with a case study. This is the story of what happened to Andrew when he tried to use his assertiveness to put forward a case for a pay rise.

Case study 5: Andrew

Andrew works for a small, privately owned company that stocks and distributes solvents and lubricants. Andrew is employed as Office Manager and he has been in this position for the last two years. He is now 33.

Before he became Office Manager, Andrew worked on accounts and credit control for four and a half years. He was asked to take the job of Office Manager when the previous incumbent left under a cloud and the Managing Director (the owner of the business) needed someone who could fill the slot quickly. He was given a modest salary increase and told that his package would be reviewed again once he'd demonstrated that he could do the job.

In this respect, Andrew feels he has done well. His predecessor failed to address a number of problems with staff over the years and Andrew was left with the task of having to sort them out. Finally, when everyone in the office was performing satisfactorily, Andrew carried out a complete overhaul of the order processing procedure, meaning that customers now have a next-day delivery service on any stock items (a vast improvement on the targets that were achieved previously).

What Andrew finds slightly disappointing, however, is that the Managing Director has not raised the subject of his salary again. The year-end salary review came and went and Andrew received the same percentage increase awarded to everyone else. Because of the size of the company, Andrew sees the Managing Director almost every day of the week and there have been plenty of opportunities for a discussion to take place.

Andrew is not pushy by nature, preferring, on the whole, to soldier on with his work quietly and to lead others by example. Ideally he did not want to have to confront the Managing Director and remind him about the promise to look at his salary he made two years ago, yet he feels he is left with no choice.

Picking a quiet moment after hours one night when most of the staff have gone home, Andrew asks the Managing Director if he can have a word with him. When they're seated privately in the Managing Director's office, Andrew wastes no time in getting round to the subject he wants to discuss. He tells the Managing Director he feels he's demonstrated his ability to perform effectively as an Office Manager. Now it's time his efforts received the recognition they deserve. As to the promises he made to him when he originally took the job, Andrew expresses his disappointment that these seem to have been conveniently forgotten.

It is this last remark that seems to anger the Managing Director. What does Andrew mean? Is Andrew accusing him of being underhand? If so, perhaps Andrew should come straight out and say so.

Andrew hesitates. Frankly he didn't expect the Managing Director to react in this way. He tries to retract by saying his remark wasn't meant in the way it was taken, but the Managing Director is still rattled and all further attempts Andrew makes to get the discussion back on track are met with stony stares. Finally the meeting closes with the Managing Director telling Andrew that there's no money left in the budget for salary increases and, like everyone else, he will have to wait until the end of the year.

Statements that invite negative responses

The key points to pick out from this case study are as follows:

- Andrew is someone who seems to have made a good job of his lifelong interview.
- From what we know of him he is an achiever who has got stuck in and produced results that have outshone his predecessor.
- Everyone in his company is presumably aware of this and, since the company is small, this must include his boss, the Managing Director. He should therefore be seen as an asset to his company – someone his boss would want to keep focused and motivated; someone he would be sorry to lose.

- For these reasons, Andrew has substantial silent bargaining power and he should be able to exercise this in the form of leverage on his boss, getting him to listen to and go along with his ideas (i.e. give him a rise).
- Andrew has made no bones about his salary disgruntlement and he communicated his disgruntlement to his Managing Director.

So where did Andrew go wrong? He simply made a statement that invited a *negative* response – an accusation that angered his boss and, as a result, the issue of his salary got sidetracked.

Key point

Steer clear of making statements that invite negative responses. As in Andrew's case, it could be the reason why your assertiveness doesn't work. Rather, you must ensure that any communicating you do is put within an entirely positive framework. In this way it stands a chance of producing the result you want.

Notepad

We will be coming back to Andrew a little later in this chapter when we will be giving him a second chance to present his case for a pay rise.

Don't whine

Accusations and accusatory language are types of communication that invite a negative response. There are others – let's deal first with whining.

How do we avoid being seen as a whiner?

- **Don't** harp on ancient history. If you've been treated shabbily at some point in the past, leave it there (in the past). Dragging out old scores gives the impression of someone who harbours resentment. This won't help you when it comes to getting people to listen to you and take your ideas and opinions seriously.
- **Don't** preface statements you make with a negative, for example: 'My career isn't moving very fast and I want to talk about my prospects for promotion.' The first part of the

sentence adds nothing to what you want to say, and carries the risk that any subsequent discussion will be about whether you are making slow progress or not.

- **Don't** use words such as 'unreasonable' or 'unfair'. Try to talk in facts rather than apply value judgements that other people may not share.
- **Don't** make statements that could suggest you are envious – for example: 'People in the New York office get a luncheon allowance.'
- **Don't** bring up a problem without offering a solution.
- **Don't** repeat yourself.

Don't make threats

Assertiveness and making threats sometimes get mixed up. Threats are yet another example of statements that invite negative responses. Someone who feels under threat will often react in a way you're not expecting. Take the case of Paul:

Case study 6: Paul

Paul is the Contracts Manager of a company in the heating, ventilating and air conditioning industry. He is 46 and he has been Contracts Manager for the last seven years. His total service with the company is just under 15 years.

Paul has been locked in an argument with his management colleagues for some time over whether the company should be tendering for work overseas. The Sales and Financial Managers are both in favour of moving into what they see as lucrative new markets in Eastern Europe and the Mediterranean. Paul, on the other hand, feels that the company doesn't have the capability in terms of skilled engineers and support personnel to take on more and more contracts over an increasingly wide geographical area and where local conditions may prove to be difficult. What's more, Paul realizes that, as Contracts Manager, most of the problems will land on his desk and, for this reason, he feels his opinions should be taken into account.

The recent signs are, however, that Paul is losing the argument and, at the last management meeting, the CEO, Greg, seemed to be definitely siding with the Sales and Financial Managers when the subject of tendering for overseas business came up. Disturbed by what he saw as his opinions being ignored, Paul asked Greg for a private meeting. During the course of this meeting, Paul tried again to get Greg to see the difficulties that could arise from trying to manage several contracts spread all over Europe without the right staff infrastructure in place. Greg listened, but Paul could tell by the way he kept shaking his head that none of the points seemed to be making any impact. More disappointingly, when Greg did speak he simply churned out the argument that no business could afford to stand still and, if lucrative markets were opening up in other countries, it was his job as CEO to see that the company exploited them. As to difficulties in running contracts, Greg's only comment was that there were always difficulties and it was up to management to find ways of overcoming them.

Feeling prickled by this last remark, and the way Greg had effectively dismissed his arguments, Paul played his final card. He would resign if this went ahead, he said. He could not be party to a decision which would draw the company into a bottomless pit of problems that at some stage would impact on profitability and threaten the futures of all of them.

Clearly stunned by these words, Greg sat back in his chair. He asked Paul whether he meant what he had just said and, when Paul said yes he did, Greg suggested they adjourn the meeting for 24 hours to give everyone a chance to cool off.

Next day Greg called Paul into his office. This time the mood was stiff and formal and, without any preliminaries, Greg asked Paul whether he had changed his mind about what he had said yesterday. Paul said he had not. He would resign if the plan to tender for overseas business went ahead. Greg shook his head and said he was sorry because he valued Paul as a Contracts Manager. However, he could not let his feelings for people come in the way of doing what was best for the business and, on that basis, he was going to recommend the Sales and Financial Managers' plan to the Board.

Don't use threats to back up assertiveness

Paul is now in a position where he must either:

- carry out his threat to resign, or
- back down.

Resigning may not be what he wants to do – not really, not with nearly 15 years' service with the company. And if he backs down, this will have a negative effect on his self-esteem and make him less certain when it comes to exercising assertiveness again in the future.

What's interesting about Paul's case study is that he intended the threat as a hammer blow – if you like, the ultimate weapon in his exercise of assertiveness – with the aim of getting his boss, Greg, to sit up and take notice of what he was saying. The trick, however, backfired. He not only lost the argument, he also put himself in a very difficult position.

Warning

Don't make threats unless you're prepared to carry them out. Always think through all the implications of anything you say.

Notepad

Remember, silent bargaining power is based on *implied* threats rather than anything that passes from your lips. It is the thought in the other person's mind of what you might do if they fail to attach sufficient importance to your ideas and opinions that exerts the leverage.

Don't put forward negative arguments

Apart from making a threat, where did Paul go wrong? With 15 years' service with the company and seven years in the job of Contracts Manager it seems safe to assume that his views and opinions would have value in the eyes of his boss and his colleagues. So why did they choose to take little notice of him? Why did his assertiveness fail to work?

One reason why he didn't make much impact could be to do with the fact that the argument he put forward was entirely *negative*. In essence, he was saying that the idea of developing an overseas customer base was completely out of the question. Not surprisingly, perhaps, none of his colleagues found this very persuasive, because, as his boss quite correctly pointed out, no successful commercial enterprise can be based on the principle of standing still. How could he have done better with his argument? Though we're obviously not acquainted with all the facts, a far more appealing way of presenting the same case would be to say something on the lines of, 'Yes, we could spread the customer base overseas but, before we do, we need to recruit and/or train X new engineers and support staff. It will take Y months and the cost to the company will be £Z.' The trick is, you will note, to turn the negative into the positive, and the result, hopefully, is that people will be more prepared to listen to you.

Key point

Only argue cases you can win.

The power of spoken communication

Having looked at what *not* to do when communicating verbally – avoiding statements that invite negative responses – let's now turn our attention to what we *should* do. How can you be more assertive in your spoken communication? What does it take?

Plan what you're going to say

If an opportunity is about to present itself to put forward your ideas and opinions (for example, a meeting) dedicate a little time to thinking through what you're going to say. Preparation is where many people go wrong when it comes to delivering assertiveness. Effort put in at this stage usually pays off enormously.

Have an aim

Though it sounds pretty obvious, you need to start with an aim. What are you seeking to achieve? Here a good tip is to identify a single aim. For example, if we go back to case study 6 (Paul), his aim could be to get proper funding for the recruitment and training of staff in his department. Where life could start getting complicated for him is if he tries running a second aim alongside his main aim – for example, an aim to scupper the Sales and Financial Managers' plan to tender for business overseas. Not only is the second aim negative, it could come into conflict with his main aim. The mixed messages could be picked up by Paul's boss and it won't be clear whether he is advancing a genuine argument or whether he's just playing a game of office politics. This will undermine the plausibility of what he is saying.

Communicate the aim

This is what it's all about – sharing your thoughts with others and doing this in such a way that others will take your ideas and opinions to heart.

What are the strong points in your arguments?

Take a sheet of paper and write down all the reasons you can think of why other people should be convinced by what you're going to say to them. When you've finished your list, go through it and pick out the three reasons that stand out as the most convincing. Mark them with a highlighter pen.

What's the purpose of this exercise? People on the whole are not blessed with very long attention spans so anything you say has got to be said in a relatively compressed period of time. Once this period of time has elapsed people's attention will start to wander and you will find you have lost your audience.

Key point

Keep it short. Keep it concise. Keep the attention of those you're seeking to convince. Don't find that your audience has switched off before:

- you've finished;
- got to the best part.

Clarity

Clear and concise communication is easily assimilated and understood. Someone who is clear commands attention. Someone who is not confuses people to the point where they give up listening because they feel they haven't followed, or they simply can't be bothered any more.

How to achieve clarity

- Use words that everyone understands. Don't, for example, use jargon unless you're certain that the people listening to you are just as familiar with the jargon as you are.
- Keep sentences short. Don't go off into a long string of clauses and sub-clauses that will have everyone trying desperately to remember what it was you said at the start so that they can make sense of it all.

- Without it sounding silly, speak slowly (practise with a friend or record your voice on a tape).
- Don't drop your voice at the end of sentences. It's a habit many of us have and it makes it harder for people listening to follow what you're saying.
- Resist the urge to 'dress it up'. Sometimes we do this when we're concerned that our audience won't find what we're saying very palatable. Bear in mind that obscuring the message in this way can obscure the meaning. Best to stick to 'telling it straight'.

Notepad

Will it help you to be more assertive if you can increase your vocabulary to include words that are not in common everyday usage? Will it make you look more educated? As a result, will it lift your image in the eyes of others and add importance to your ideas and opinions?

In the question and answer section at the end of this chapter we offer further advice on this (see p. 58, 'Word power').

Prepare for the dialogue

The spoken word is special in that it's normally delivered face-to-face or over the phone. Reactions to what you say are immediate. You say something, someone says something back, you respond and a dialogue ensues. It is the quality of your performance in this dialogue that determines how successful you are going to be in getting others to accept your ideas and opinions. In other words, a good clear and concise statement of where you're coming from won't be enough on its own. What you also need to do is have enough ammunition to keep the argument going.

From a preparation point of view, this means making an intelligent guess at how individuals are going to react to anything you say. For instance, will they take the opposite viewpoint or, from what you know of them, is it reasonably safe to assume that they will be on your side? Anticipating the reaction extends to anticipating how the reaction will pan out. What arguments are certain people likely to employ? Use your knowledge of them to predict the direction they will be coming at you from. Then, most importantly, think out the arguments you are going to use.

How to handle discussion

To sum up so far, you are now at the stage where:

- you know what you want to say;
- you know how you're going to say it;
- you're prepared for what people are going to say back to you.

To illustrate these points, let's go back to case study 5 (Andrew) at the beginning of this chapter. Andrew, you remember, was looking for a salary increase for what he regarded as rightful recognition of his input. He came unstuck because he made a remark that invited a negative response from his Managing Director. For this reason his assertiveness failed.

Now let's give Andrew another chance. Let's send him to see his Managing Director again and see if he can make a better job of handling the discussion about his salary.

Case study 5 (continued): Andrew

Prior to going to see the Managing Director, Andrew gives some thought to what arguments he is going to use to support his case for an improvement in his salary. First on the list is the promise the Managing Director made to him when he took the job. Why hasn't the promise been met? Andrew can only speculate on the reasons although he has a sneaky suspicion that the Managing Director is suffering from a convenient lapse of memory. The Managing Director has many virtues as a business man but he is notoriously tightfisted when it comes to money.

Realizing immediately that reminding the Managing Director of his promise will only serve to put him on the defensive and could sound like a gripe, Andrew decides instead to set himself an aim. The aim is to get his salary raised to a level that will reflect his worth to the company and, in this respect, Andrew feels his worth is quite high. His first task is to communicate this aim, and, as for presenting his case, Andrew decides to let the facts speak for themselves:

- He's been in the job two years.
- At the start he had a lot problems to sort out (problems that he tackled).
- He has introduced new systems.
- The company operates more efficiently as a result.
- He deserves recognition in the form of more money in his salary packet.

How will the Managing Director react? Because of his inclination to be tightfisted, Andrew is confident that the Managing Director will come up with some reason why he can't offer more money. How to respond? Andrew figures it would be best not to let the discussion get too bogged down in arguments about the extent to which the Managing Director's hands are tied by financial constraints. Andrew decides he must make the Managing Director realize that:

- he's no pushover (he'll stick up for himself if he has to);
- he's serious;
- he won't go away;
- if his aspirations aren't met, he could decide to take his talents elsewhere.

Let's pause the action there to take a look at how Andrew has prepared himself for his meeting with the Managing Director. The key points to pick out are as follows:

- Even though he feels aggrieved about the Managing Director's convenient oversight of the promise he made two years ago, Andrew correctly takes the view that raising the subject with him now will invite a negative response. For this reason he decides not to mention it.
- He decides instead to put forward a quick five-point case for why it would be appropriate to give him a pay rise.
- He anticipates the Managing Director will use financial arguments to say why a rise can't be paid.
- Correctly, he spots the dangers of getting side-tracked into financial arguments (an area in which the Managing Director has greater knowledge by virtue of his position, and on which it would be difficult to challenge him).
- Importantly he sees his silent bargaining power as the best weapon at his disposal and, with silent bargaining power, the fewer the words, the better.

Now let's go back to the story and see how Andrew gets on in his face-to-face meeting with the Managing Director.

Case study 5 (continued): Andrew

After exchanging a few pleasantries about the day's happenings, Andrew comes straight to the point. He is extremely happy in the position of Office Manager, he tells the Managing Director, so happy that he intends to carry on doing the job to the best of his abilities and build a future with the company. He has one problem, however, and that is the problem of his pay. He feels he deserves a better salary and these are his reasons (the five bullet points).

The Managing Director clears his throat before replying. He is the first to appreciate the good work he has done for the company, he tells Andrew, and it was his intention to do something about his salary sooner. Sadly, however, his hands have been tied by budgetary constraints. There is simply no extra cash to go round on salary increases other than the percentage norm awarded to everyone at the end of the year.

Andrew says he fully understands budgetary constraints and that trading conditions have been difficult for the last two years. In this respect, he and other managers must continue in their efforts to make the company more efficient and thereby ensure that profitability is maintained. As to how his rise can be afforded, he will have to leave the matter in the Managing Director's hands. He adds as a parting shot that it is a pity that this one item is casting a shadow over his otherwise complete satisfaction with his employment with the company.

Whether Andrew's silent bargaining power will work for him or not remains to be seen, but what he has achieved in this meeting with his boss is as follows:

- His aim has been communicated clearly and concisely. The Managing Director is now under no illusions as to the way Andrew feels.
- He has achieved the above without making threats or saying anything else that could invite a negative response. Indeed, by making it clear that he is happy in his role with the company, he has taken a positive step towards removing any impression that he is making a threat.
- He has made it clear that his aspirations are confined to a single issue (his pay), and that once this issue has been addressed, his aspirations will be satisfied. This will (a) help focus the Managing Director's mind and (b) reassure him that Andrew isn't harbouring a number of grudges, i.e. conceding on one issue isn't going to lead to the raising of others.

- He has used his silent bargaining power effectively. The leverage is now working on his Managing Director. By communicating his aim in a plain and forthright manner, the Managing Director is now fully aware that if he doesn't do something for Andrew he runs the risk of losing him and having to find a new Office Manager in a few months' time. This prospect won't appeal to him one bit if Andrew is doing a good job. Also, the bad memories of Andrew's predecessor will still be fresh in his mind.

Putting it into writing

Most people are reasonably comfortable with the spoken word, but it's a different matter when it comes to expressing their ideas and opinions in writing. The reasons for this seem to range from uncertainty about their powers of self-expression and knowledge of grammatical constructions through to a reluctance to put anything in writing that could be brought out and used against them in the future.

Why put it into writing?

As far as this book is concerned, our interest in written communication is confined to the extent to which it can be used to reinforce our assertiveness.

Though it is true to say that the use of written communication has declined over the last 25 years, mainly due to advances in telecommunications technology, with the advent of e-mail and text messaging, it could be said that written communication is making a comeback. Where people once picked up the phone or paid a visit to someone's office, they now send them an e-mail or text instead. More traditionally, however, written communication tends to be used in the following situations:

- where spoken communication isn't an option – for example, where you need to communicate with someone who doesn't live locally and you can't find their 'phone number;
- where the subject matter is sufficiently important for there to be a need to put it on record;
- where you're confirming something – for example, confirming a price you've given to a customer on the phone;
- where the subject matter is complex and requires lengthy explanations, or where spoken communication would be impractical and/or there would be a risk of people switching off out of tedium.

The force of written words

A point always to bear in mind is that written words have a force. The fact that they're there in black and white, staring up at you from the page, gives them an added feel of importance. For example, Andrew, in case study 5, could have followed up the meeting with his Managing Director by sending him a letter or an e-mail confirming the main points of their discussion. Whether it would be wise to do this or not is a different matter, particularly in a small company where (a) people don't normally resort to sending letters to one another and (b) letters received in this way could be viewed as threatening. On the other hand, what is quite certain is that a letter or e-mail received from Andrew would have left his Managing Director in no doubt as to his seriousness. It would add a further dimension to his assertiveness and this is an important point to consider.

Key point

Remember the force of the written word. It can add weight to your arguments just by its presence.

Grammatical concerns

This is an important item to address because a whole section of society is deterred from putting anything into writing because they lack confidence in their ability to express themselves in correct grammatical forms. They worry that they could come across as uneducated and this will make it harder to get others to see them as people whose ideas and opinions should be taken seriously.

Warning

Software such as spell checkers have taken much of the pain away for people who don't feel comfortable with their ability to use language correctly. Don't rely on these innovations too much, however, because they can and do let you down – for example, you might use a correctly spelled word in the wrong context, or give it the wrong meaning. The advice on the next few pages will help empower you in your use of language.

Use a dictionary

Even if you're working with modern word-processing software, keep a dictionary on your desk and get into the habit of checking the spelling of any words you're not too certain about. At the same time check whether the word means what you think it means. Remember that spelling and word usage gaffes will damage your image as someone whose ideas and opinions are important and to be trusted.

Avoid complex grammar

If there's a problem, always seek to go round it rather than run into it head on. In the case of grammar, this means avoiding anything that has the potential to get you into trouble. Here are three tips:

- Don't over-use punctuation. Colons, semicolons and commas in text denote pauses of different lengths and there is a temptation to pepper them all over the place. Try to avoid this because it can have a disconcerting effect on anyone reading what you've written. Try as far as possible to stick to simple full stops to break up your flow of words.
- Keep sentences short. Remember the greater the use you make of subordinate clauses, the greater the chances are of you getting it wrong.
- Try to stick to three tenses: present, past and future. Keeping your sentences short will help you achieve this.

Self-expression

Another obstacle to putting it into writing is the fear many people have about their ability to express themselves. Try to make friends with words and shed any inhibitions you may feel about using them. Good writers tend to express themselves in the same way that they speak, and this is an example you should try to follow. Write down what's in your head quite literally, and let the words flow out. The first few times you try to do this may not be perfect, but you will find that you will soon start to iron out the creases and writing will become a much more natural activity for you.

Warning

Don't feel inhibited to copy the formalized or affected styles of writing used in many business letters. Don't feel constrained by the need to express yourself in a certain way. Worry more about giving rein to your thoughts than to conforming to conventions. Most conventions are outdated anyway.

Improve your self-expression skills

We have already touched on the benefits to be gained from reading more widely and, in particular, from making it a habit to read a good-quality broadsheet newspaper. There is a further spin-off from improving the quantity and quality of your reading. You can see how good writers express themselves and you can learn from them. As you read, try at the same time to get into the language of the writer and see how it is used.

Improve your word power

At the same time as working on your self-expression, you can use your wider reading to improve your word power. Here is how to do it:

- Use your dictionary to find out the meaning of any new or unusual words you come across.
- Start a word list by writing down any new words and their meanings in a notebook.
- Spend ten minutes a day testing yourself randomly on the words in your word list.
- Try to make it fun by, for example, having a competition each day with a friend or colleague (making it fun will help you to stick at it).

If you follow this plan, you will be surprised how quickly your word power starts to improve.

Warning

Don't be tempted to use words in written communication that are not completely familiar to you until you are absolutely sure of their meaning. Remember, anything in writing is there for the record and your image as a competent credible person is at stake.

Key point

Greater fluency in word usage adds to the impact of any message you're seeking to put across, and this applies irrespective of whether the message is being delivered in written or spoken form. People listen and take note of those who can express their ideas and opinions using language with flair and confidence. Importance is automatically attached to anything they say or have put down in writing.

Body language

As we noted earlier in this chapter, what makes spoken communication special is the fact that most of it is transmitted face-to-face. So, in assessing the impact of the message we're putting across in spoken communication, we need to consider not just what people hear with their ears but also what they see with their eyes.

Body language is another form of communication. In our posture, in our facial expressions, in the way we use our hands we send out messages to people and these messages give a further dimension to our words. For most of us, however, this use of body language is an involuntary act. As we speak we're not aware that our faces are creased in a frown or that we're waving our hands in the air. By the same token, if anyone told us to correct our body language we would find it hard to do. The end result, in many cases, would be a heightened feeling of self-consciousness and, needless to say, this wouldn't do our confidence much good.

Threatening body language

As we've seen, threats are usually counterproductive when it comes to putting forward assertive arguments. The party on the receiving end of a threat often reacts:

- in a way you're not expecting;
- negatively.

Threats can come across in body language – for example, the wagging finger held up in front of someone's face will serve to put them as much on the defensive as a barrage of threatening words. The use of threatening body language is something to be avoided for the simple reason that it won't help you to assert your ideas and opinions. Here is a short checklist of some of the more common forms of threatening body language:

- jabbing, stabbing fingers;
- tightly clenched fists;
- using hands and fists to strike hard objects, e.g. banging your fist on a table or desk to give emphasis to some point you're making;
- bone-crushing handshakes;
- space invasion (getting too close to people);
- touching (other than a standard polite handshake);
- scowls;
- staring, glaring eyes.

Assertive body language

Acres of print have been devoted to the subject of body language, ranging from the useful to the outlandish and, frankly, weird. Before getting too concerned by the various messages our bodily movements and postures convey, it may be best to remind ourselves what we're seeking to achieve from our assertiveness: to convince others that our ideas and opinions are important enough to be given serious and proper consideration. What you're seeking to do therefore is impress on whoever is listening to you that:

- you're not a threat;
- you know your stuff;
- your ideas and opinions can be trusted.

How can body language contribute to this process?

- Try to remember to smile when you're talking to people. The natural inclination will be for them to smile back. Immediately a rapport is struck and their defences (if they have any) will melt away. (Note: you can practise smiling at people and see how this natural inclination to smile back works.)
- If the person you're talking to is a complete stranger or someone you only meet occasionally, then a handshake may be appropriate. Remember to grasp not too firmly and not like a wet lettuce either. Shake for a few seconds then release. Your handshake is intended to reflect friendliness and impart a feeling of trust. It is not a test of strength (a signal to the other person that you could be seeking to dominate them). Similarly, by not over-prolonging it, you are not being too familiar or outstaying your welcome.

- Keep your hands away from your face when you're talking, as this not only makes it harder for the other person to hear what you're saying, but it can also create the impression that you're trying to conceal something and that what you're saying can't necessarily be trusted.
- Think 'open'. Open hand gestures with palms extended outwards (towards the person you're addressing) send out a strong message and show that you've got nothing to hide. Facing the other person, as opposed to standing or sitting sideways on with your shoulder towards them says much the same thing. Incidentally, the latter can also give the impression you're half-interested or being stand-offish.
- Don't stand too close to the other person or invade their body space. In office situations the presence of a desk or table between the two of you helps in this respect.

Warning

What about turning up the volume of your voice a notch or two? By being louder won't it help you be more assertive?

Understandably most people would feel hesitant about suddenly affecting a resonant, booming voice. True, your friends and colleagues would take note but, at the same time, they would probably think you'd taken leave of your senses. Their trust and confidence in you and your ideas and opinions would be undermined by what they saw as strange behaviour. The message? Never do anything you're not entirely comfortable with, and don't think that by speaking louder you're being more assertive.

Notepad

With communicating and assertiveness, what works well in one situation won't necessarily work well in another. We have already commented on small organizations and how written communication may not be favourably received simply because it's not the usual way of doing things. Indeed, in such organizations, 'putting it into writing' could even be construed as a threat thereby inviting a negative response. In Chapter 6 we will be looking at how assertiveness needs to take account of situations and people. Applying a 'one size fits all' approach can lead to assertiveness backfiring and the ramifications for you, the user, can be unhelpful.

Questions and answers

Threats sometimes work

Q *I work in sales and I have seen a number of my colleagues do very well for themselves by asking for rises and threatening to leave if they don't get them. What do you say to this?*

A The people you're talking about have obviously got substantial leverage and, because we're talking about sales, it seems a safe bet that this leverage is based either on their performance or on the amount of business they could take to a new employer, or on both. The mistake, however, is to assume that everyone has got the same leverage so, if it was in your mind to follow in their footsteps, you need to ask yourself first whether your departure would inflict as much damage on your employer's business as theirs. Also you need to take into account that companies sometimes get fed up with being blackmailed and make a decision to take a stand. In other words, you might not have any joy with your threat to leave and you need to reflect on where this could leave you (out on the job market where you may not want to be or, if you stay, with a big dent in your credibility). The bottom line here is to repeat the advice never to make threats unless you fully intend to carry them out.

Part of the furniture

Q *I've been with my company a long time and I find sadly that I don't get the same ear with higher management as some of my younger colleagues do. I am approaching 57 and I guess one of the reasons why no one attaches too much importance to my opinions and ideas is the fact that I'm not likely to leave. To use your terminology, I don't have any leverage and, more to the point, there doesn't seem to be a fat lot I can do about it. Any comments?*

A Yes, quite a few. First, don't write yourself off in terms of silent bargaining power and leverage simply because of your age and long service. Although we don't have any details on your seniority and job function, we can only assume that your departure from your company has the potential to inflict considerable damage on them and this, if you remember, is the way to measure silent bargaining power. For example, you've probably got a lot of experience and knowledge locked up inside your head and this could be the kind of experience and knowledge that would be useful to competitors. Also they might find it hard to replace you if you decided to leave at relatively short notice and these are all factors that in normal circumstances, would serve to exercise leverage. So your problem, we suspect, is one of credibility rather than silent bargaining power. No one has ever seriously considered you leaving (not really), so no one takes too much notice of you. You're viewed as part of the furniture and this is a situation many people with long service with an employer find themselves in. What can you do about it? Somehow – and without resorting to threats – you've got to get it over to your higher management that the idea of leaving doesn't frighten you. So, perhaps the next time you feel no one is listening to you, what you need to do is make a statement on the lines that you like your job, you like working for the company and you would like to see your time out to retirement – indeed the very last thing you would ever want to do is go off and work for someone else. However, you do have these concerns about the treatment given to your ideas and opinions and you would like to see a bit more recognition all round, etc. What you will have achieved in this sort of presentation is the restoration of your credibility. You will have sent out a message that you won't put up with being treated like part of the furniture any more and you're looking for attitudes to change. Note that in cases like yours this message may need repeating a few times before it sinks in. The ultimate test is of course the strength of your silent bargaining power, but in this way at least you're giving it a chance to work for you.

Word power

Q *Will it impress people if I use long or unusual words? Will it help me to sound better educated?*

A No and, more to the point, you could end up looking foolish if you're not normally given to using long words and/or you're not too sure about their meaning. If you want to extend your word power then follow the advice given in this chapter.

I get tongue tied

Q *I never seem able to express myself very clearly. Do you have any advice for people like me who get tongue tied?*

A For a start, don't worry, because worrying only makes matters worse. Getting tongue tied usually arises because you're trying to express too many thoughts at the same time. The remedy is to see if you can break down what you want to say into a series of short simple sentences (the less the better). Try practising this technique and you will find the benefits are almost immediate. Knowing when to shut up is also a great help. Remember, the signal to stop talking is flashing at you as soon as you've delivered the message you want to put across. Take heed of it and don't undo all your good work by going off into a long repetitious ramble where your tongue really will tend to go into big tight knots.

Summary

We can have the most wonderful ideas and opinions in the world, but we won't convince anyone else that they're wonderful unless we have the ability to communicate them properly. In this chapter we have looked at communicating in its three forms – spoken, written and body language. We have seen with each of these forms how it is possible to achieve greater assertiveness by focusing on the way we present our messages. In particular, we have seen the dangers of presenting our messages in ways that automatically invite negative responses. People don't like being threatened or dominated and, sadly, a lot of assertiveness techniques such as loud voices, knuckle-crushing handshakes and staring-out competitions have precisely this effect. To accept the point of view that you're putting across, the other person has got to feel comfortable with you and this won't happen if your method of communicating is in itself the cause of unease.

Communicating your ideas and opinions is something you can always get better at. It is a process of continuous self-improvement that goes hand in glove with your own personal development, as you gain a better appreciation of life and understanding of others. An important point to remember is that a good communicator is also a good listener, and appreciating where the other person is coming from (his or her ideas and opinions and the extent to which they're in line with or at variance to yours) will be the basis for any success you are going to have with assertiveness. This leads us to our next chapter, where we are going to look at assertiveness in the context of people and situations. Notably we will be looking at where, when and how to use assertiveness and, given the people and situations, what works and what doesn't.

04 the power of judgement

In this chapter you will learn:

- **the importance of taking people and situations into account**
- **how, where and when to use assertiveness**
- **where assertiveness can get you into trouble**

Taking people and situations into account

To recap, so far we have looked at three of the four foundation stones of successful assertiveness:

- you;
- what you know;
- how you put it across.

Now we are going to turn to the final foundation – the power of judgement, by which we mean the power to judge how, where and when to use assertiveness taking into account people and situations. Once again, let's look at a case study to draw out the main points – this time the case study of Delia and Mark.

Case study 7: Delia and Mark

Delia is a senior account executive with a firm of advertising agents and Mark, the Managing Partner, is her boss. The firm is based in a provincial town and it has built up its business within the local market where recruitment advertising and advertising for estate agents and car dealerships makes up a substantial part of the turnover. Mark and his two partners started the firm five years ago. Delia joined shortly afterwards with a brief to develop sales of recruitment advertising (a field in which she had considerable experience with one of the well-known names in the industry).

Most of the time Delia and Mark get on fine. There has been a steady growth in recruitment advertising business since she joined and this has led Mark to form a positive view of Delia's worth. For her part, Delia finds Mark a reasonable person to work for. He is fair, sometimes a bit volatile, but, on the whole, good at running the business and managing his staff.

At ten o'clock one morning a fax arrived just as Delia was leaving the office on her way out to make a presentation. The fax was from one of the firm's top clients. It contained copy for a recruitment advertisement that the client wanted to appear urgently in the jobs supplement of the next day's edition of the local newspaper. The copy needed setting up properly in the client's border artwork, then faxing to the newspaper in time for the 2.00 pm deadline for next day copy – all tasks Delia would normally have looked after herself. Now, however, with the presentation to go to, Delia had to find someone in the office she could delegate the tasks to, and here she ran into the familiar problem of everyone being 'too busy' to help. Finally, with the clock ticking away and with some misgiving, she gave the fax to Cassie, the office junior. She asked Cassie to get the Production Department to set the advertisement up in the client's border style, then when it was in its finished form, to fax it to the newspaper in advance of the 2.00 pm deadline.

It was after 6.00 pm when Delia got back to the office. Apart from the partners who were locked in a meeting, everyone else had gone home.

Next morning Delia had to take her car in for a service meaning she arrived just after 11.00 am. She was met by Mark, red in the face and demanding to know where she'd been. Not waiting to hear the answer, Mark then told her he'd just spent an unpleasant 20 minutes being given a roasting by the client's Chief Executive. It seemed there was no sign of the advertisement in the jobs supplement of the newspaper and the client's Chief Executive was demanding to know why. What's more he was prepared to take his business elsewhere if no satisfactory explanations could be provided.

Sensing that something had gone seriously wrong and that Cassie was most likely to be at the bottom of it, Delia asked Mark for 15 minutes to make a few enquiries. Mark grunted. He said he hoped she could come up with some good excuses because he'd promised to phone the client's Chief Executive back within the hour.

Finding Cassie at her desk, Delia asked her point blank about the fax. Cassie replied that she'd taken it down to the Production Department exactly as Delia had instructed but nothing had come back. Did Cassie think to chase the Production Department? Cassie said she didn't and that in any case she didn't think it was her job.

Delia grimaced as she made her way back to Mark's office via the Production Department where she found the client's advertisement set up and lying in an out tray. Mark went ballistic when he heard what she had to say. He wanted to know what Delia was playing at entrusting the important business of a leading client to the most junior employee in the firm. He would talk to her later, he said, but first he'd got a big smoothing-over exercise with the client on his hands.

Smarting from the interview, Delia went back to her office. Mark had got this wrong, she kept telling herself. She had had a presentation to do and delegating the client's advertisement to Cassie was the only option for her. The fact she had no proper back-up was hardly her fault. She'd simply been trying to do her best and Mark needed to be told this. Indeed, if anyone was to blame it was probably Mark for not ensuring the office was staffed with sufficient competent staff.

When assertiveness is best forgotten

Here then we have a challenge for Delia's assertiveness. She is about to be reprimanded by her boss, Mark, for abdicating responsibility for looking after an important client's business. How should she respond? The assertive side of her is suggesting that she should be firing back by telling Mark she wasn't abdicating but trying to do her job with the few resources available to her. However, let's pause for thought for a moment so we can consider Delia's position in a little more depth. In particular, let's consider the extent to which Delia's position might be considered weak:

- There is no evidence in the case study that Delia took the time and trouble to impress on Cassie the importance of getting the client's copy faxed over to the newspaper by 2.00 pm. The impression is that Delia shot off in a hurry to do her presentation, giving Cassie the bare outline of what was required and no inkling of the importance of the task that had been delegated to her.
- Certainly there is no evidence that Delia made it clear to Cassie that it was up to her to chase up the Production Department.
- It seems Delia already had misgivings about Cassie's competence. In which case, what was she doing entrusting an important task like this to her in the first place?
- Given that Delia did delegate the task to Cassie, why didn't she ask a senior colleague (for example, Mark) to keep an eye on things in her absence?
- Could Delia have checked up on Cassie herself by making a phone call rather than leaving events to fortune?

In assessing these weaknesses in Delia's case, we can anticipate what might happen to her if she starts getting assertive with Mark. A bad situation could get a whole lot worse. Mark, it seems safe to say, wouldn't take too kindly to being lectured by Delia for a breakdown in communications that was largely her fault. He would be even less impressed by the suggestion that he was in some way to blame. In short, a standard telling-off for Delia could turn into a blazing row with no knowing what the outcome might be.

Key point

Know when it's best to:

- forget assertiveness;
- lie down and take the flak.

People who are on your side

Getting assertive with people when you're on weak ground is one situation where the warning bells should be sounding off at you to think twice. Another equally inappropriate use of assertiveness is in situations where there is no need for it because the people you're talking to are already on your side. Indeed, subjecting a favourably disposed person to a bombardment of assertiveness could have exactly the reverse effect to the one you intend. It could serve to put questions in their minds (questions that weren't there previously). At worst it could cause them to distrust you and turn them against you.

Key point

Being assertive is all well and good but it can backfire on you and this is why you must always put aside a few moments to consider the likely impact of your assertiveness before you put it to the test. Could it end up with you on the wrong end of a weak argument? Could it serve to put people's backs up?

When you are too close to a situation and not able to see a way forward too clearly, a good way of examining the likely consequences of your assertiveness is to enlist the help of someone you trust and whose judgement you respect, for example, your partner. Ask them what they think. Could you be putting yourself on a road of no return? Could you be in danger of alienating people who could normally be counted on to be backing you? If so, the signal to you is to stop in your tracks.

Knowing when to use assertiveness

To sum up, because of the need to take people and situations into account, assertiveness should never be seen as a general purpose tool to be employed in all situations. Rather it should be used *selectively* and in a way that is appropriate to the people concerned and the task in hand.

The test of importance

In deciding whether to use assertiveness, the first question to put to yourself is how much importance you attach to the issue you're facing:

- Will it impact directly on you?
- Does it matter to you if the ideas and opinions of others prevail over yours?
- Is it something you're prepared to fight for?

By putting these questions to yourself you can test how much the issue really means to you. Assertiveness is hard work and placing a lot of effort into a cause which has little significance as far as you are concerned and/or doesn't really interest you doesn't add up. More to the point, the *stamina* you need to keep your assertiveness going will have a natural tendency to flag if the outcomes aren't important to you.

Key point

Pick issues you care about when you decide to make a stand. Make the distinction between what's important to you and what isn't.

Who to be assertive with

We've already pointed out that being assertive with people who are on your side is not necessary, and can sometimes backfire.

However, what about the rest of humanity? How do you determine who you need to be assertive with and who you don't?

For a few clues on how to proceed with this, let's go back to case study 7 (Delia and Mark). The advice to Delia, remember, was to think twice before trying out her assertiveness on Mark. She was largely in the wrong over the incident of the fax and arguing her (weak) point of view with Mark seemed destined to get her into even more trouble than she was in already.

Consider the character you're dealing with

There is a further point to consider with Delia and Mark, however, and this is the nature of Mark's character. Mark, we are told, is essentially a fair-minded person who has a tendency to go off the handle occasionally but who, by and large, seems to be receptive to logical and reasonable arguments. Delia seems to have a problem with the level of support available to her in the office and whether she wishes to make an issue out of this is something she needs to decide by applying the test of importance. Given that she decides that lack of support is an impediment to her in carrying out her function as a senior account executive (and feels this is an issue that needs to be addressed) then she has to decide how best to proceed. Here is where the power of judgement comes in. How would it be best to broach the subject with Mark?

How to proceed

Clearly it would not be advisable to take issue with Mark when he still has an irate client to deal with and when his own temper is also frayed. A discussion on the lines Delia is planning would be best left to a moment of calm when the dust has had time to settle.

> **Warning**
>
> Don't be assertive with someone who isn't in the mood to be receptive. Timing is important. Pick the right moment.

In presenting her case to Mark, some of the points Delia needs to consider are as follows:

- Delia should not say anything that could invite a negative response. She should put everything in a positive framework and avoid making accusations, threats and statements that could come over as complaints, for example Mark is to blame for not staffing the office properly.
- She should use her knowledge of Mark to determine how best he can be persuaded to accept her point of view.

- She should consider that, in his case, she will be talking to someone who has a vested interest in the success of the business and that the most convincing arguments will be those that point the way to greater success in the future.
- It appears she has substantial silent bargaining power. She is in a high-profile position and she has a good track record for bringing in business. As a consequence she has considerable leverage on Mark. We can presume that he wouldn't want to see her leave and he would probably be the first to appreciate the damage she could do if, for example, she went to work for a competitor. In short, given that Mark is restored to a more equable frame of mind, he will probably take note of anything she has to say and treat her ideas and opinions seriously.
- She has the power of knowledge on her side. She has experience of the recruitment advertising business going back over many years and it is reasonable to suppose that she knows more than Mark about what life with clients is like at the sharp end.

Delia shouldn't have too much difficulty convincing Mark that better arrangements need to be in place to give her support, hence there should be no need to bring out the big guns to get him to hear her out. Hopefully, all that will be called for will be a short discussion pointing out how much more effective she could be if she had proper back-up in the office – followed by a few suggestions, for example designating a competent member of staff to whom she can delegate tasks when she has to go out on business.

Key point

Always take into account the personality you're dealing with. Use your judgement to determine the form that your assertiveness should take. Most importantly don't let your assertiveness be the reason for your arguments foundering.

Warning

When dealing with people like Mark, who are not only the boss but also owners of a large slice of the equity in the business, there is a danger that assertiveness used in a heavy-handed manner could be read as an attempt to usurp their authority. Tread warily when dealing with people who may be hypersensitive to challenges and people who are insecure or lacking in confidence.

Cracking tough nuts

Someone like Mark is probably going to be a relative soft touch when Delia wants to get her ideas and opinions heard. But what about people who aren't so amenable? What about people who won't listen or who are downright awkward or hostile? Let's look at another case study to see what you need to consider when you have to deal with tough nuts.

Case study 8: Phil and Lester

Phil is a Factory Manager. He works for a company that makes plastic injection mouldings mainly for use in the telecommunications industry. He is 38 and has been in his job for the last six years. Previously he was employed by another plastics injection mouldings company where he worked in a technical capacity (designing production equipment and moulding dies).

Over the past five years, Phil's company has been through hard times – partly due to the depressed state of the market and partly to the influx of cheap plastic injection mouldings from the Third World. A consequence of these difficult trading conditions has been several episodes of headcount slashing, culminating last year in the removal of the entire supervisory tier. Since the factory works three shifts 24 hours a day this has left Phil with a very difficult situation to manage.

Phil reports to Lester who is a vice president of the parent company. Lester is responsible for all European operations and he is known for his hard-nosed, no-nonsense approach. It is Lester who has been the driving force behind the cost-cutting programme and it was his idea to strip out the supervisory tier – a decision on which Phil feels his views were not given proper consideration. Whilst Phil was fully appreciative of the need to reduce overheads, he saw that quality would soon become an issue without a supervisory presence on the production shifts. He made these views known to Lester and pointed out that there would be problems with customers if standards were allowed to lapse. Lester's retort was that some other way would have to be found to get round quality, but offered no solutions. When Phil pressed the point, Lester snapped back that, as Factory Manager, it was Phil's job to come up with solutions – not his.

Let's stop the action there for a moment to take stock of how Phil has performed so far:

- Phil is clearly competent and can talk authoritatively about plastics injection mouldings. He has been in the industry a long time. He has a good technical background – the power of knowledge is on his side.
- We can only assume that he carries clout with his seniors and that he should be able to exert leverage through his silent bargaining power.
- He seems perfectly capable of putting his case to his hard-nosed boss – communicating his ideas doesn't seem to give him any difficulty.
- His argument for retaining the supervisory tier may be sound but it is negative and fails to address the overriding need in the company which is to reduce costs in the face of falling markets and increased global competition. Unsurprisingly perhaps his argument makes no impact on Lester.

Now let's go back to the case study

Case study 8 (continued): Phil and Lester

It was not long before Phil's assertions about quality were proved to be right. Two months into the new unsupervised production arrangements, there was a complaint from a major customer about a consignment of work that had been despatched from the night shift. Phil eventually managed to smooth things over, but the cost to the company of replacing the faulty consignment was considerable and Phil reflected glumly on how the expense of employing a supervisor on nights faded into insignificance in comparison. What's more, there were three similar incidents in the weeks that followed and several times Phil found himself on the point of picking up the phone to tell Lester that his cost-cutting ideas had backfired badly. This, he fully realized, wouldn't go down too well but, what was concerning him greatly, was the undermining of customer confidence and the long-term effect this would have on the business. Most of all, he realized the company couldn't stand any further loss of business. However, he also realized that people at the top of the organization like Lester had bigger fish to fry and the likely reaction to any loss-making subsidiary would be to close it down rather than think too closely about their own flawed decisions. No, Phil told himself, if the business was to be put back on track then he, Phil, would have to be the driving force.

Let's interrupt the action again to say Phil is correct in his reading of the situation. He was right in his appreciation of the quality situation but to tell Lester 'I told you so' would gain him nothing except a short-lived and worthless feeling of self-satisfaction. The issues here are clearly very important to Phil. His future is at stake along with the future of everyone else employed in the company. Somehow he's got to convince Lester to think again. How can he do this?

Case study 8 (continued): Phil and Lester

Over the years Phil has got to know Lester well. That he is a smart operator is beyond any doubt, though his rise through the ranks is largely attributable to his toughness and single-mindedness. What Lester is certainly not good at is admitting that he is wrong and Phil realizes that, in this respect, he needs to tread carefully.

A further consideration is that Lester sold the board on the idea of delayering the plastics injection mouldings company by taking out the supervisory tier, and to have to do a U-turn in front of the President and his colleagues would go completely against Lester's nature.

Straightaway therefore Phil realizes that he will have no joy whatsoever in persuading Lester to go back to employing a team of supervisors. Where he does have a card up his sleeve, however, is that he could, at a push, operate the factory on a two- rather than a three-shift basis and make up any shortfall with overtime. The shift to go would be the night shift with some of the personnel affected absorbed into the two remaining shifts. The advantages to Phil would be as follows:

- Most of the quality problems had occurred on the night shift for the simple reason that the night shift was the shift with least contact with managerial and technical staff (who work normal office hours).
- Mainly because of shift payments, lighting and heating bills, and the need to provide out-of-hours maintenance cover, the night shift is by far the costliest shift to operate hence there would be savings that would more than offset the cost of any overtime.
- A quality presence could be maintained by managerial and technical staff during normal office hours, meaning absence of cover would be confined to approximately four hours in the evening. Phil figured he could get round this difficulty by taking on a part-time quality technician to work evenings only. The

overall cost of employing such a person would still be well within the overall level of savings generated by closing the nightshift.

- The total plan would be 'sold' to Lester as a cost-cutting measure.

Strive for common ground

We hope that Phil is successful in getting the quality standards in his company back on track and that customer relations are restored to normal soon. The point to this case study, however, is to illustrate how, when dealing with tough nuts like Lester, it's important:

- to avoid conflict;
- to try to see where the other person is coming from;
- by seeking out the common ground, to use arguments that he or she is going to find acceptable.

Key point

People may not always find your arguments convincing for the simple reason that they are proceeding from a standpoint that is entirely different to your own. Try to:

- fathom out their standpoint;
- rearrange your arguments;
- assert yourself by coming at them on the same wavelength.

Questions and answers

The test of importance (1)

Q *In my job there are a whole range of issues which don't affect me directly but where I feel, nevertheless, that I could still make a valuable contribution to the discussion. With your test of importance, are you suggesting I should be keeping quiet on such issues? If so, isn't this likely to reduce my standing with my colleagues i.e. a bad effect?*

A Deciding whether to speak out on subjects that don't affect you directly should be subject to a two-tier test:

- Are you competent to talk about the subject?
- Does it interest you sufficiently to enable you to carry your arguments forward convincingly?

Before getting too hung up on definitions of what's important and what isn't, keep focused on the fact that assertiveness is an empowering tool, not one that's put there to cramp your style. Providing the two tier-test is met, feel free to express your ideas and opinions on any subject you like and, as you say, your standing with your colleagues should improve.

The test of importance (2)

Q *An issue that surfaced recently is the downsizing of my company car. My firm was sold out to a competitor last year and the new owners are seeking to impose less advantageous job terms on my colleagues and I. The reason, we're told, is to iron out anomalies and bring us into line with the rest of their staff. In my case, the bone of contention is my company car which is up for renewal shortly and which is going to be replaced by an inferior model. Needless to say, I am not very pleased about this for two reasons:*

- *The car is part of my package and I don't think the new owners have the right to downsize it without my agreement.*
- *The kind of car I drive is important to me.*

I feel that this is an issue I must make a stand on but what do you think?

A Legally speaking, you may be right in your assertion that the new owners need to get your agreement before downsizing your car, but pause for thought just for a moment because there are bigger issues at stake for you here and ones that you need to consider carefully before doing anything. The period following a takeover, merger or acquisition is usually quite tense and not normally the best time to be sticking your head up over the parapet. Having said this, any joy you're going to have with negotiating a special dispensation for the model of company car you operate is going to depend on your silent bargaining power with the new owners. Are there big upsides for them in keeping you motivated and 'on board'? Alternatively, are you and your car-shaped happiness of little concern to them? Remember, in forming this appreciation you will be looking at the new owners' relatively limited experience of you. It is a mistake to base your assumptions on any kudos you had under the previous regime. More importantly, perhaps, you should be trying to see where the new owners are coming from in seeking to impose these less favourable terms on you. Anomalies cause problems in organizations and, if you and your colleagues enjoy substantially better terms then the new owners' existing staff then, somewhere along the line, trouble is bound to surface. In short, the new owners may have little choice other than to seek to bring your terms into line and this means the chances of making you an exception are probably:

- remote;
- only likely if the stock of your silent bargaining power is very high indeed, for example you have knowledge locked inside your head without which the firm would find it hard to function.

Use the advice given in this chapter to present arguments that:

- are positive;
- stand a chance of finding favour with the new owners because they start from the same standpoint as theirs.

With regard to the second bullet point, the same standpoint means recognizing the problems that can be caused by anomalies and putting forward an argument that addresses these concerns. For example, could you say to the new owners that you appreciate their difficulties but there's a difficulty for you too in seeing one of your most cherished perks taken away? Could you explore ways of softening the blow, such as a one-off compensation payment? With this kind of approach, you're joining in the debate with the new owners rather than engaging in conflict at the outset.

Summary

Assertiveness will work for you, providing you use it:

- on the right people;
- in the right situations;
- in the right way.

The *power of judgement* is seeing that there is more than one way of being assertive and tailoring the technique to the task you face. There is no 'one size fits all' approach and appreciating this is a key part of any success you are going to have.

part two

applying assertiveness

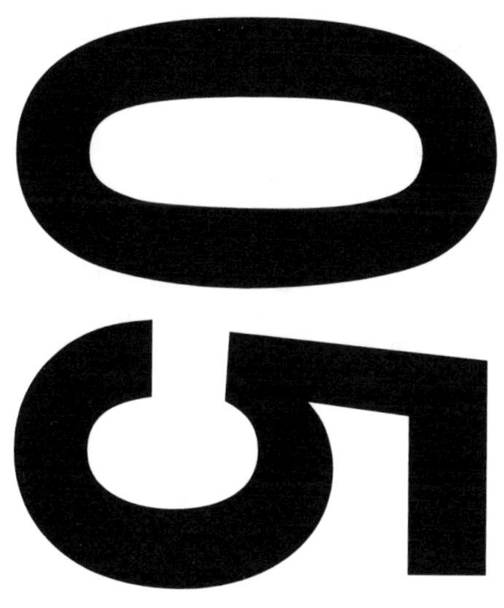

05 assertiveness in business

In this chapter you will learn:

- **how to make your voice heard in business decisions**
- **what your colleagues and contacts will make of it**
- **how to handle their response**
- **how to use assertiveness in small businesses**
- **what to do when you work for yourself**

Influencing outcomes and decisions

Assertiveness in business is about:

- making a bigger and more significant contribution;
- seeing your views and opinions prevail over others;
- enabling you to influence outcomes and decisions.

To see what's involved, let's look at another case study. This time it's the turn of Elaine and Ralph. Elaine is seeking to influence a decision which she believes will have an important bearing on the business she manages. Ralph is her boss.

Case study 9: Elaine and Ralph

Elaine is the manager of a High Street employment agency where she has worked for the last nine years. The agency supplies temporary office staff to a range of clients most of whom are located within a 15-mile radius. Apart from Elaine there are four other people employed in the agency.

The original owner of the agency was Kay. Kay managed the business herself until five years ago when she slowly started to take a back seat. Just over three years ago she promoted Elaine to manager and effectively retired from day-to-day involvement in the running of the business so that she could pursue other interests. Last year, however, Kay announced to everyone's surprise that she was going to put the agency up for sale and, two months ago, new owners arrived in the shape of a holding company with interests in property development, hotels, tourism and leisure as well as employment agencies.

At first Elaine's relationship with the new owners went well. Ralph, the CEO of the holding company, struck her as someone she could do business with.

However, the issue that caused Elaine not to see eye-to-eye with Ralph was that of the agency's trading name. Since Kay founded the company 15 years ago, it had always traded under the name of Kaytemps. As Kaytemps it had built up an excellent reputation in the area for the quality of the service it provided to its clients, and this is what had given it the edge over its competitors (and at the same time enabled it to charge higher prices). Now, six weeks into the new ownership, Ralph had written to Elaine saying he was in favour of getting all the employment businesses in the group to trade under the same name – consistent, he said, with developing a single brand image that would form the basis for future development and acquisitions. The name he suggested was the name of one of the other agencies owned by the group (the largest in terms of sales turnover, but not a name that would be recognized by any of Elaine's customers).

Elaine reflected on what she should do. Ralph, of course, had no experience of the temporary staff recruitment business and, short of sitting in her seat for six months, there was no way he could ever appreciate the sheer volume of competition she had to deal with every day – ranging from the big names down to small fry who came and went but who still had the capacity to take business if the opportunity presented itself. A change of name, she reasoned, would have no benefits and would only serve to sow seeds of doubt in customers' minds – seeds of doubt that a service they were hitherto perfectly happy with was, in some way, going to change and probably change for the worse. No, Elaine decided, somehow she'd got to persuade Ralph to drop his idea and to keep the Kaytemps name.

So, is Elaine right in her assertion that a change of name will inflict damage on the business? Only time will tell of course, but as the manager of Kaytemps, she is certainly well placed to make the assertion – better placed than her new boss Ralph, for example, or, for that matter, anyone else in the organization. For this reason alone her opinions should carry weight and get a hearing. But how should she proceed?

Rate the chances of your success

In business you don't win all the arguments and you need to accept that your assertiveness skills won't always carry the day for you irrespective of how well you use them. Take Elaine's case. What she doesn't know at this stage is how firmly committed Ralph is to the idea of a single trading name for all the employment businesses in the group. Is it something he's effectively made his mind up about already? Or will a strongly argued case based on potential loss of business serve to sway him? Elaine will only find out the answers to these questions when she has broached the subject of retaining the agency's name with Ralph. Are there any indicators as to how he is going to react? Here Elaine is at a disadvantage because her knowledge of Ralph is based on a very short acquaintance. How she reads him could therefore be flawed. The sensible course would be to err on the cautious side and to see this first test of her assertiveness skills on Ralph as an expedition into unknown territory. The outcome could go in her favour but, there again, it could go against her simply because of Ralph's character.

Notepad

It could be that Ralph has decided there is no way he is going to perpetuate the name of the previous owner in the trading title of the business. If so, it would put Elaine in the position of backing a loser from the beginning. Nothing she is going to say will persuade him to change his mind. She needs to allow for this eventuality.

Why it's important to rate your chances

Given this unpredictability when it comes to business decisions and how they're made, it pays (always) to go through the process of making an assessment of what chance you have of influencing the outcomes at the start. Unlike Elaine, you will usually have some insight into the characters you're dealing with and what drives them. You will know, for example, if they have any pet schemes or where your ideas and opinions may come into conflict with theirs. If the character happens to be the decision-maker (for example, your boss) you can thus form a view on what joy you are going to have with influencing the outcomes of the decision your way.

Why is this so important? For the simple reason that it will help you identify lost causes before you put too much effort into them. Also you need to bear in mind that lost causes don't always look like lost causes at the outset. The true extent of the hopelessness of a case sometimes only becomes apparent as you move your arguments forward – this could be a situation that Elaine will find herself in. The watchword here is *flexibility*. We will have more to say about flexibility later in this chapter.

Key point

Don't go round banging your head on brick walls. It's painful as well as pointless.

How much silent bargaining power do you have?

In assessing the likely impact of any business arguments you put forward, a further factor to take into account is how much silent bargaining power you have. Silent bargaining power, you remember, manifests itself in the form of the leverage you can bring to bear on those you are seeking to influence and persuade. You will find your audience more receptive to what you are saying if you have an abundance of silent bargaining power on your side.

In business, nine times out of ten, the person you will be seeking to influence and persuade is your boss. We saw in Part One how to measure how much personal clout you carry by doing the 'leaver' test. Would your boss miss you if you went off to work somewhere else? Alternatively, would they be rubbing their hands with glee at the prospect of being rid of you? Asking yourself questions such as these and answering them honestly will give you a feel for how far your bosses will be prepared to stretch themselves to accommodate your ideas and opinions. If you are a key player in the organization with talents that will be difficult to replace then, rest assured, mountains will be moved to keep you sweet and 'on board'. On the other hand, if you are known across the organization as a trouble-maker or someone who puts in less than full effort then the reverse will apply (the shutters will be put up).

On the face of it, Elaine wouldn't seem to have a problem with her silent bargaining power. As incumbent manager of Kaytemps with the ex-proprietor now well and truly off the scene, she would seem to be in the position of sole key player in the business with all the levers that make it a success firmly in her hands. For this reason it seems fairly safe to assume that she would be sorely missed if she decided to take her talents elsewhere. In short, Ralph would appear to be heavily dependent on her for the continuing healthy performance of his new acquisition (something he would not want to jeopardize).

Ownership

Rating your chances of success is all well and good, but to a large extent you will be making inspired guesses. Whether these guesses are right or not, will only be proved one way or the other when you put your assertiveness to the test. This brings us to a difficulty. Once voiced in a business context, our ideas and opinions take on the status of our personal property. As such, we protect them to the best of our ability and, whilst this is mostly for the good, it can work against us in situations where the outcomes we are pursuing cease to be attainable (realistically speaking). For example, if it became clear to Elaine that Ralph's idea to change the name of the business was really an entrenched opinion on which he was unlikely ever to change his mind, then the sensible course would be to review her opposition to the idea on the grounds that it may get her nowhere apart from banging her head on a brick wall. The difficulty is, of course, that ownership and the passion associated with it occasionally drive us to carry on past the point of no hope, and herein lies the danger. Remember the importance of flexibility and how it is vital not to get yourself locked into lost causes irrespective of how justified they may seem to you at the time. Tune yourself to pick up when the argument may be drifting away from you – when the time has come to disengage.

Notepad

Pursuing lost causes can lead you into territory you never envisaged at the outset. In the question and answer section at the end of this chapter we deal with the options you face when business decisions go against you (see p. 92, 'When is it a resigning matter?')

Prepare your arguments

Here we go back to the advice in Part One of the book. In particular:

- Give some time to preparing the arguments you are going to use to put forward your case.
- Focus on the need to use arguments that invite positive responses.
- Anticipate any counter-arguments.
- Have your answers ready.

Put your case

Having decided whether oral or written communication is more appropriate, always set out to make your case in the clearest and most concise terms possible. In business there is little room for frills and you won't win any bonus points by rabbiting on *ad nauseum* about your ideas and opinions while everyone else slowly switches off. Here the principal issues are clarity and credibility. Everyone needs to know:

- exactly where you're coming from;
- what you're seeking to achieve;
- that you know what you're talking about;
- that you mean it.

Listen to what others have got to say

Business is built on team effort and performance, and so it is important that you:

- take into account the ideas and opinions of others;
- see this as part of your assertiveness.

What this means in practice is saying to everyone 'this is what I think but I want to know what you think too'. Listening is a great art but sadly very few people seem capable of doing it properly. Good listeners benefit enormously in terms of their ability to:

- understand others;
- incorporate their ideas and opinions into their own.

What you must also allow for is that people you work alongside in business (bosses, peers, subordinates, external contacts) often have valuable contributions to make. This is especially true of people whose experience and knowledge is wider than your own. Embellishing your ideas and opinions with the ideas and opinions of the people you are seeking to convince will serve to make them stronger and more acceptable.

Key point

Don't see business assertiveness in terms of winning battles by the brilliance of your intellect or the sheer force of your personality because real life isn't like this. Yes, your ideas and opinions may sometimes have sufficient cutting edge to wow everyone into stunned appreciative silence, but don't expect this to happen too often. Most people have minds of their own and they won't be happy until they've told you what they think. In other words expect a dialogue to ensue from your assertiveness and don't see it as a threat. Instead view the ideas and opinions of others as a source of enrichment. Learn to pick out the good parts from what they have to say and do this by listening to them properly. The object, remember, is to bring the team with you not to lose your colleagues' support or make them feel they've lost the argument and thereby estrange them from the process of carrying your ideas and opinions forward.

Warning

Remember that assertiveness is not about acquiring a brash new image that (a) you won't be comfortable with and (b) could turn you into an object of ridicule and put dents in your credibility. Nowhere is this truer than in business. Colleagues will be quick to notice changes in behaviour and put their own interpretations on them. Needless to say, most of these interpretations won't be very flattering.

Getting results

Going back to case study 9 (Elaine and Ralph), we saw how Elaine set herself the task of talking Ralph out of changing the name of Kaytemps using the argument that it would result in a loss of business and reduced profitability. Convincing? It would seem so, yet Ralph may have already considered this eventuality and decided to run the risk anyway because greater benefits would accrue in the long term from all the employment businesses in the group trading under the same name. Clearly if Elaine engages in a dialogue with Ralph she will learn more about what's behind his thinking and she may, as a result, drop her opposition to the idea. For example, she may see the benefits for her personally in being part of a bigger, more united management team in a growing organization. In short, by staying flexible and hearing out Ralph's point of view she could change her stance completely and do this from a position of strength and without any undercurrent of feeling that she has 'lost' the argument.

Key point

Seeing someone else's point of view and accepting it should never be seen as weakness. You won't always be right and one of the benefits of giving a proper hearing to what colleagues have to say is that you can identify where their ideas and opinions are better thought out than yours.

Let's say, however, that Elaine was right in thinking that Ralph had failed to appreciate the realities of operating in the tough commercial world of employment agencies. Let's say that her dialogue with him revealed that he was expecting Kaytemps to go on making good returns under its new name. What should Elaine seek to do next?

Winners and losers

A facet of business life is that relationships between people often extend over long periods of time. Even when individuals have left organizations, it is not unusual to find they keep in contact with ex-colleagues. A large slice of professional networking is built around these long-term relationships.

When it comes to our dealings with bosses, peers, subordinates and external contacts, we can't build successful relationships on being right all the time while the other person is always in the wrong. Sooner or later we will acquire the reputation of being know-alls and for this reason people simply won't want anything to do with us. The same goes for winning all the arguments and putting the other person in the position of being the loser. No one likes being a loser. More to the point – and as we noted previously – someone who feels they've lost the argument won't be inclined to be too supportive when it comes to putting your ideas into action.

So what's the answer here? Simply this: as part of your business assertiveness you need to keep people who've conceded the argument on side. How do you do this?

- by treating their ideas and opinions with respect throughout;
- by extending this respect to listening carefully to everything they have to say;
- by conceding arguments where the issues are no longer important to you;
- by conceding arguments you can't win.

With the last two points, the suggestion is to adopt a 'win some, lose some' approach to influencing business decisions, and this will generally help you to maintain good relationships with your colleagues. The arguments you need to win are those where the issues are important to you. Any that are less important to you, you can afford to concede.

Notepad

Problems with assertiveness are shared by a large number of people. Not everyone you come into contact with in the course of your professional life will be proficient when it comes to putting forward arguments. Here is where you could provide a helping hand. When engaged in a dialogue with a colleague you could ask questions to ensure that you understand fully what the other person is saying. Displaying this level of interest in someone else's point of view will go a long way towards removing areas of conflict and smoothing the way forward. If they have to concede the point then they will be more inclined to do so gracefully and without any antipathy towards you.

Bring silent bargaining power to bear

Going back to Elaine, she could be working for Ralph for a long time and, since he is clearly well placed to have a major say in how her future career progresses, she needs to be careful how she tells him that his appreciation of what market conditions are like in the employment industry is wrong. At one extreme, coming to blows with Ralph over an issue such as this could put a serious rift in their relationship. At the other, not making the point forcefully enough could result in the change of name plan going ahead with the consequent loss of business and Elaine's head being put on the block at some stage in the future for failing to deliver the results. What should she do?

1 Without voicing any opposition, Elaine should find out what's driving Ralph. Does he have some big vision? Could he share his thinking more fully with her? With more information Elaine has the option to voice her support for the plan if what she hears is to her liking – adding the qualification of course that there is a risk in the short term of loss of business arising from the agency having to trade under a new and unfamiliar name. To keep the conversation positive it would be useful from Elaine's point of view to have some proposals ready for countering loss of business – for example, bolstering up the sales effort for a fixed period by taking on temporary personnel.
2 If she is still left feeling that the plan is ill-conceived, Elaine needs to voice her concerns by letting the facts speak for themselves – how the agency operates, the nature of the competition, the link between the Kaytemps name and the

agency's ability to charge higher prices and ultimately the added value that this generates. The suggestion to Ralph is on the lines that, yes, she understands where he's coming from but why rock the boat?

3 If Ralph is still adamant about the change of name then, rather than get into another round of arguments, Elaine should seek to bring the meeting to a close. In doing this she needs to keep the tone cordial and positive right to the end.

4 Let the silent bargaining power take over. Ralph is now aware that Elaine isn't happy with his proposal. He is aware too that one of Elaine's options is to take her talents elsewhere. If this concerns him (if silent bargaining power is on her side) then he will think twice about imposing a decision that is not to her liking. He will see the damage that her leaving could inflict and he will back off. How he dresses this up is, of course, very much up to him.

Ralph is still the boss, however, and there is no guarantee that Elaine's assertiveness will yield the result she is seeking. What she has done, however, is:

- put her case forward;
- given her silent bargaining power a chance;
- not soured the relationship with Ralph.

How colleagues react

Moving on with the theme of how the people you work with will react to you being more assertive with them and its importance, let's look at another case study. This time it's the turn of Fay, a Manager who is having problems with one of her staff.

Case study 10: Fay and Joanne

Fay is an audit manager with a firm of chartered accountants. She was promoted into this position six months ago and it is her first management job.

Joanne is a junior auditor who works for Fay. In recent weeks Joanne has started arriving late for work. At first she was just a few minutes late, but over the past fortnight her timekeeping has worsened. She is now arriving 15 to 20 minutes late most mornings.

Fay realizes it is her job to make sure that her staff come to work on time. However, she has never had to discipline anyone before, and having to have words with Joanne is not something she feels very comfortable about.

Fair enough, Fay is new to the job of management hence the prospect of having to take someone to task for an aspect of their performance is not one she is either familiar with or looking forward to. Yet Fay's choices are limited. To leave Joanne's conduct uncorrected isn't a viable option and could result in Fay getting into trouble with her seniors for not doing her job properly. On the other hand, there is Joanne's reaction to consider. Fay has probably never had to assert herself in a disciplinary sense before and how Joanne is going to view this is hard to say. For example, she may view it as Fay picking on her and being unfair. As a result:

- her reaction to any warning she is given is likely to be negative;
- her effort will go into finding further fuel for her growing sense of injustice rather than getting to work on time.

Gauge the reaction

Gauging how people will react to you being assertive with them is nothing more than applying a little common sense to your existing knowledge of them, and the case study of Fay and Joanne illustrates this. What it also illustrates, however, is the difficulty you might face where your colleagues (bosses, peers, subordinates or external contacts) may find your assertiveness strange or out of character. This is mostly likely to happen where, like Fay, you have never previously had the need or inclination to exercise assertiveness. Joanne may, for example, feel resentful about being told by Fay to pull her socks up and get to work on time. She may see this as Fay trying to pull rank on her or getting too big for her boots now she's been promoted. In short, the purpose of the exercise (getting Joanne to mend her ways) could get lost because Joanne will be too wrapped up in a sense of injustice to see the point Fay is trying to make.

How to handle negative reactions

Never apologize for speaking plainly because, once you do, you are on the slippery slope to dismantling your most compelling arguments. Instead emphasize the gains to be had from greater openness:

- better understanding of where everyone is coming from;
- more fruitful dialogue;
- greater chance of reaching a satisfactory resolution.

You also want the other person to be open back. Do they agree with you or do they have a problem with anything you've said? If so, what is the problem? Can they please explain?

The aim here is to get any negative sentiments out in the open where you can deal with them – for example, to get Joanne to say she feels she is being used as a scapegoat, so that Fay can tell her, she's wrong. The alternative (saying nothing and letting her bad timekeeping continue) would not be consistent with looking after her best interests. Far from being an exercise in victimization, the aims in speaking to her are (a) to find out what's causing her to come in late, (b) to see what can be done to put matters right and (c) to agree a way forward.

In reality you may find it hard to get people to voice their deeper misgivings about your assertiveness, so you may have to:

- guess at the misgivings (based on your knowledge of the person);
- pre-empt them by making a statement (see list above).

Key point

Don't back off from being assertive with work colleagues just because you're worrying about how they're going to react. The new you may seem strange to them at first but:

- they'll soon get used to it;
- over a period of time you'll gain their greater respect.

Notepad

A reminder that in Chapter 4 we looked at situations in business where it is best to forget assertiveness and keep your head down – notably situations where:

- you're in the wrong (you're arguing from a position of weakness);
- the odds are stacked against you (you won't win).

Assertiveness in SMEs

We're constantly reminded that the business landscape is changing and more and more of us work in organizations that employ fewer than fifty people. So, from an assertiveness point of view, what is different about working in an SME (small- to medium-sized enterprise)? What special considerations need to be taken into account?

Everyone knows everyone else

Relationships between people in SMEs are very different from those that are found in the bigger companies. Everyone knows everyone else. There are few barriers. Structures are relatively informal.

Silent bargaining power in SMEs

This is where people who work in SMEs score. Silent bargaining power can be brought to bear right across the organization. For example, everyone from the CEO downwards will know:

- the value of your talents;
- the size of the clout you carry.

This means that if your stock is high in the organization you have the capacity to exert leverage at all levels. Remote figures won't have to be persuaded to take your ideas and opinions seriously.

Working for yourself

Today an increasing number of people work for themselves, and they range from the traditional self-employed sector (sales agents, freelance journalists, plumbers, painters and decorators, etc.) through to the new breed of professionals who make a living selling their expertise wherever they can find takers. What can greater assertiveness offer to people who work independently? To help answer this question, let's take a look at another case study.

Case study 11: Louise

For just over four years Louise has worked as a freelance IT trainer – a career she took up when she was made redundant from a position as a Secretary/PA with a large insurance company. Today Louise sources most of her work from the same company. When she became qualified as an IT trainer, she tapped into her networks among former colleagues and, because of her reputation for being reliable and good at her job, she was given a chance to prove her worth in a new role as an outside service provider.

Everything has gone well for Louise as far as the training of her old employer's staff is concerned. She has received many messages of thanks and appreciation and the demand for her services has increased threefold since she first started. However, there is one fly in the ointment. The fee Louise charges has never changed because she does not want to rock the boat by putting up her prices. For example, where would it leave her if her old employer decided to take its IT training business elsewhere? How would she be able to plug such a big gap in her earnings? Yet her costs keep rising and Louise realizes sooner or later she will have to face up to taking some decisions.

Who's got the muscle?

So what are we looking at here? Someone who's good at what she does but not so good when it comes to business and being assertive? Or the age-old problem of placing too much reliance on one big customer who can then effectively call the shots?

Yet Louise's case study illustrates a more fundamental point about people who work for themselves. They are small (by definition) but the people they do business with (their customers and their suppliers) don't necessarily fall into the same category. Indeed, we can sometimes be talking about quite sizeable organizations with a lot of power to their elbow when it comes to negotiating terms and prices. At least that's the way it looks to someone like Louise as she seeks to escape from the squeeze on her profit margins. As for assertiveness, Louise has already written it off for the reason that she feels she is not in a strong enough bargaining position. Good thinking? Maybe, but before leaping to any firm conclusions about where she stands with her big customer and how assertiveness could come to her help, she needs to reflect a little further.

Size isn't everything

In any business situation, how well your assertiveness will work is largely determined by how much silent bargaining power you have on your side. Silent bargaining power is the expression of your value or worth in terms of:

- what the party on the receiving end of your assertiveness stands to lose if you decide to take your talents elsewhere;
- what in turn makes it in their interests to give proper consideration to any arguments you put forward.

Louise has formed the view that she doesn't have much going for her in the way of silent bargaining power, but is this true? Louise, it appears, is doing a good job as an outside training provider and her client might not find it easy to replace her with someone of the same calibre. What's more, this is something they probably know. Added to which is all the hassle that goes with changing to someone new – plus the problems that will arise if the someone new doesn't work out. In short, what we could be looking at here is a long list of highly compelling reasons why Louise's big client would want to do their utmost to keep her on board. No silent bargaining power? Louise clearly needs to think again. Our advice to her? To go for it and make a case for increasing her fees. At the same time, stop feeling grateful to her big client. They need her just as much as she needs them.

Key point

Don't see working solo as a position of weakness when it comes to being assertive with people you have to do business with and who are bigger than you. The real measure of your clout is your value to these people – size doesn't come into it. Work on your value. See your silent bargaining power as your biggest asset.

Questions and answers

When is it a resigning matter?

Q *What happens when an issue is vitally important to you and you don't get the outcome you're looking for? Is it ever a resigning matter?*

A Resignation is clearly a very final gesture and some would say the measure of last resort when it comes to facing up to business decisions that go against you. Yet the real point to focus on with resigning isn't so much the principle that's at stake but the question of method and timing. Contrast handing in your notice in a fit of pique with planning your exit from an organization deliberately and carefully. With the first you may get a short burst of satisfaction from telling your bosses what they can do with their job, but the ecstasy may turn out to be short lived. Soon you'll be plunged into the harsh reality of having to find something else that will generate sufficient cash to keep the wolf from the door and it may not be easy. Indeed, you may be forced into the position of having to accept the first reasonable offer that comes along and, needless to say, this won't necessarily be consistent with the all-round advancement of your career. On the other hand, with the second (the planned approach), you can make your exit at a time of your choosing and this would normally be when you've found another good job to go to. The fact that you're looking is something you keep to yourself.

Throwing in the towel

Q *In the case of Elaine (case study 9) are you suggesting that she should give into to her boss Ralph if he is adamant about changing the business's name? If she is right that the business will suffer, then this won't do anyone any favours – notably her.*

A What we are saying is that there comes a point where continuing to voice an opinion becomes an exercise in futility – for example, where the other person has effectively made his or her mind up and stopped listening some time ago. In such circumstances it's important (a) to stop because you are effectively banging your head on a brick wall, and (b) to take stock. Given that the decision that's gone against you is flawed and, as in Elaine's case, could have damaging consequences, then it may be worth waiting for the dust to settle before giving your assertiveness another (final) try. Any further lack of progress should be read as a sign that your silent bargaining power isn't going to work and a suggestion perhaps that the time has come to start thinking through your options generally.

Going over the boss's head

Q *When is it right to go over the boss's head? When you're not happy with a decision that's been made, should you be expressing your opinions to someone higher up the ladder?*

A Going over the boss's head is clearly a high-risk game and one you should only enter into with your eyes wide open. Having said this, if you're completely at loggerheads over an issue with the person you report to, then it may be best to try a consensual approach first. What this means is saying to the boss,'OK, you and I don't see eye to eye on this matter, so how about going to see the big cheese, putting our respective points of view and letting him/her make the decision?' Of course not all bosses will be receptive to a suggestion on these lines, in which case the issue of going over the boss's head effectively becomes one of going behind his/her back and this puts an entirely different light on the matter. You may win the day, but the chances are that the relationship between the two of you (the trust and confidence) will never be the same again. What's more, you may find that going to see your boss's boss doesn't have the outcome you'd hoped for. You may find the same line is taken, reflecting that:

- the boss and the boss's boss share the same opinion; or
- the boss's boss feels it incumbent on him/her to support the boss (irrespective of the merits of the case you're putting forward); or
- the boss has simply been acting as his/her boss's mouthpiece.

Given these quite serious downsides, a sensible way to proceed before putting your case to someone higher up the tree is to take a few soundings first. How does the land lie with the boss's boss? Could he/she be trusted to talk to you in confidence? How sympathetic to your point of view is he/she likely to be? Here your internal networks could be useful to you. Are you on good terms with anyone who is close to the boss's boss and knows how he/she thinks? Better still, do you know anyone internally who is in a position to put a quiet word in the ear of the boss's boss (to say that the boss and you are locked in a disagreement)?

Taking on more responsibilities is a mug's game

Q *I work in a small firm and my bosses would be no better pleased than to see me volunteer to take on more responsibilities. Isn't your suggestion about extending job boundaries playing right into their hands? I am certain there would be no offer of extra pay.*

A You miss the point. The fact that your bosses are happy to let you accumulate masses of silent bargaining power is to your advantage – they are playing into your hands rather than the other way round. In terms of added value, the benefits will become apparent when you exercise your assertiveness – for example, when you ask for a rise to reflect your enlarged responsibilities.

Working for yourself and being asked to cut prices

Q *My situation is not unlike that of Louise in case study 11. I am a self-employed management consultant and most of the work I do is for one company – an arrangement that has been in place for a number of years. I get on well with the Chief Executive of this company but a few weeks ago he phoned me up to say that he was asking all service providers to cut their prices by 5 per cent – me included. The reason he gave was that profit forecasts were down and somehow he'd got to demonstrate to the board of the holding company that he was taking steps to keep the business on course. He said he appreciated that no one wanted to cut their prices but he hoped he could count on me for my support. My question is what do I do? One side of me is saying don't be taken for a soft touch by being compliant. The other is telling me to go along with what I'm being asked to do because the alternative could mean no more consultancy business coming my way.*

A This is not an assertiveness issue. Supporting the Chief Executive of your client company in his moment of need takes precedence over everything else and at the same time seems like the surest way of guaranteeing his future business. In other words don't see this as you being bullied into submission by a big powerful customer because it isn't. As we've said several times in this book, assertiveness is sometimes best forgotten.

Summary

It's important to make your voice heard when it comes to business decisions, but there is no guarantee that assertiveness will work for you every time. You won't win all the arguments and knowing when to give up and concede defeat is part of being able to use assertiveness in business successfully.

In this chapter we've asked you to consider the impact your assertiveness will have on people you work alongside – your bosses, your peers, your subordinates and other people you come into contact with as you go about your day-to-day business. It's important that these people still feel comfortable with you because, if they don't, they will put up defences that will act as barriers to the effective use of your assertiveness. At worst they will take up negative postures – we saw an example of this in the case study of Fay and Joanne (case study 10).

Finally in this chapter we looked at the special circumstances of people who work in small- to medium-sized enterprises (SMEs) and people who work for themselves. With the first we saw the added scope for assertiveness in organizations that are compact enough for everyone to know everyone else. The silent bargaining power you acquire as you add value to yourself can be brought to bear right across the organization from top to bottom. Your assertiveness therefore has the capacity to transmit itself in a way that would not be possible in an organization where the people at the top are remote from day-to-day events.

With people who work for themselves we saw in the case study of Louise (case study 11) the dangers of being in thrall to big clients and feeling you have to dance to whatever tune they call. The reality is different. People who do a good job are sought after at every level and this is irrespective of whether they're employees or service providers who come in from outside. The silent bargaining power they amass is the same and they should have no fear of exercising this power from time to time.

In this chapter you will learn:

- how to be more ambitious
- how to use assertiveness to achieve defined career goals
- how to shape your own future

Ambition

We are living in the age of the self-managed career and this has been brought about by a number of factors, chiefly:

- the uncertainty that surrounds many people in careers today – the feeling that no one's job is safe in the way that it was twenty or thirty years ago;
- the disappearance of traditional paternalistic employers – the emergence of a new breed who seem to think that looking after people's careers isn't part of their remit;
- the greater value we place on personal freedom and our ability to exercise choices in the way we live our lives.

Yet this emancipation, which is what managing our own careers is all about, is something that we don't always exploit fully, and nowhere is this truer than in the way we define our ambitions. Put simply, we have a tendency to define our ambitions narrowly and, whether this arises from a misplaced sense of modesty or not, the result in many cases is that we underachieve. Can assertiveness help? Let's see.

Giving yourself the licence to dream

At the root of most people's misgivings about their own capabilities is a lack of self-esteem – a subject we looked at in Chapter 1. There we saw the benefits of tackling low self-esteem by removing the causes, notably:

- ridding yourself of negative influences, such as people who undermine your confidence;
- taking control of your life by keeping it simple and managing your finances.

Having carried out this purge of factors which could be sapping your capacity to feel good about yourself, the next step is to go to the other extreme and look at what, in a perfect world, you would really like to achieve in, say, the next ten to fifteen years. If the result of this exercise is that you come up with pretty much the same ideas that you had previously, then think again, only this time to let go properly and give free reign to some of your wilder, more fanciful dreams.

The object of this excursion into fantasy is not, as you may be thinking, to encourage self-delusion but rather to take the lid off what's going on inside your head and get it out in the open. So you want to be writing paperback fiction and getting seriously rich in the process by the time you're 30? You want to be heading up your own market leading design agency at some point in the not too distant future? There's nothing wrong with having ambitions like these even if a voice inside your head is telling you to 'get real'. You have raised your sights from where they were set previously and, for the time being, that is a sufficient achievement in itself.

Warning

Working in a job that's below your capabilities and where you are underachieving can in itself be a cause of low self-esteem. The message? Watch for the signs. If you feel you're stagnating, take control. Get off the slippery slope before it's too late.

Set your sights high

Having disposed of any tendency you may have to set your sights too low because you are lacking in self-esteem, at what level should you be pitching your ambitions? The difficulty for you here, of course, is that at the outset you may not have too much idea of what you can reasonably expect to achieve.

The golden rule is to start by setting your sights high. We say this for two reasons:

- There are more problems attached to underreaching than there are to having ambitions that are targeted too high. You could find yourself in a job that's way below your capabilities meaning (a) you've achieved nothing, and (b) you're back in the downwards spiral of stagnation and low self-esteem.
- It's easier to bring your ambitions down a notch or two than it is to go the other way.

See the full range of your opportunities

There's a big world out there and it's important you see yourself as part of it. In particular, don't define your career ambitions too narrowly, for example 'today I'm a telephone sales clerk; tomorrow I want to be a sales office team leader; in five years' time I hope to be a manager', and so on. On the face of it an approach like this looks fine, but what it fails to do is take account of the richness and diversity that modern careers can offer. It excludes opportunities rather than creates them, and this is bad. Anji is an example.

Case study 12: Anji

Anji is an assistant buyer with a small chain of retail stores. Anji's firm was recently taken over by one of its big rivals and, soon afterwards, an announcement was made that the buying department would close pending the transfer of its activities to Head Office. Anji has already been advised of her redundancy and she is currently working out her notice.

Though the rumours of a takeover have been flying round for some time, Anji is still very saddened to see her job go. She enjoys working in buying and her ambition was to use the experience she gained in her present role as a stepping stone to a more senior buying position later on. Now she feels her plans have been cut short. Her only option as she sees it is to find another assistant buyer's position – a sideways move – in order to put her career back on track. Here, however, she has hit a snag. She has been actively looking for another job for the last two months and so far she has come up with nothing. The problem appears to be a shortage of positions in retail buying and, with three weeks of her notice left to run, this is becoming an increasing concern for her.

What hasn't escaped Anji's attention is that the takeover has generated two new positions in the location where she is based. There is a vacancy for a human resources officer, and the new owners are keen to diversify into mail order and are looking for someone to come in and run it. Anji feels that neither of these positions are a match for her ambitions. What's more, she feels she doesn't have the right experience for either.

What we're looking at here is someone passing up on an opportunity to escape redundancy because she has defined her career ambitions narrowly. She may or may not be suitable for the two new positions in human resources and mail order, but there is certainly no harm in giving them a try. It goes without saying that her employer would view her applications sympathetically and this would not be the case if she applied for the same positions on the outside job market. If she succeeds in getting either of the two new positions she will:

- avoid the redundancy;
- have the opportunity to extend the range of experience into an entirely new field (human resources or mail order).

As far as Anji's ambition to be a buyer is concerned, there is no reason why she shouldn't keep going with this and do it from a position of strength with a regular income coming in. In the fullness of time she will have the choice of going back into buying or staying with her new career in human resources or mail order.

Key point

Before exercising assertiveness with the management of your career, make sure your ambitions are defined as widely as possible. In Anji's case, exercising her assertiveness on a non-existent market for assistant retail buyers would be largely pointless, whereas putting it to use across a far broader spectrum would stand an infinitely better chance of yielding positive results.

Put the right value on your talents

Questions of ambition tend to give rise to self-doubt. People ask themselves 'Am I good enough?', and usually there is no one there to provide them with the answer.

In reality there is a very fine line between realistic ambitions and those that are out of your reach. Sometimes it's tricky to define where this fine line lies. Get it wrong and you could be:

- pursuing ambitions that are below your capabilities (with all the attendant problems); or
- banging your fist on a lot of doors that don't open to you (the ultimate source of discouragement).

So far in this chapter the only advice we've given you on defining where this fine line lies is to suggest to you to start by setting your sights high – to proceed from the standpoint that you *are* good enough until there is evidence to the contrary.

Listen to the feedback

This brings us to the importance of feedback. Feedback is what gives your ambition its fine-tuning. Listen to the feedback and you will be able to pick up where there are gaps in your skills, knowledge and experience that put a certain range of ambitions out of your reach. Where do you get this feedback?

- Listen to anything that's said to you about your job performance and prospects – notably at occasions such as appraisal interviews.
- Pick up any interesting feedback from job interviews.
- Tune into your networks – see what input your colleagues and contacts can give you.

Act on the feedback

From these sources you may learn a little more about the ambitions you are right to have and those that lie outside the range of your skills, qualifications and experience. This then leaves you with two tasks:

- to tweak your ambitions accordingly;
- to identify where you could make up the shortfalls in your skills, qualifications and experience, for example by going on a course.

Warning

The important thing about feedback is that you act on it. Otherwise you will find that you are continuing to pursue ambitions that are either out of your reach or below your capabilities. Either way it won't be good for you.

Is the ambition attainable?

'Are you good enough?' isn't the only question that you need to ask in order to determine whether your ambitions are attainable. What you also need to know is whether your employer can meet your ambitions. The next case study illustrates that no two organizations are the same when it comes to having the capacity to provide people with an outlet for their ambitions.

Case study 13: Sam, Will and Emma

Sam, Will and Emma are all graduates, all in their mid-twenties, all hard-working and all with their eyes set on promotion – but there the similarities end.

Sam works for a big multinational company in the petrochemical industry. She completed the company's graduate training programme just over 12 months ago and she is now working with a senior colleague on the commissioning of a new plant in Eastern Europe. Once this project is completed she will take up an appointment at the company's head office in Germany. In the meantime she has access to a professional mentor if any aspects of the development of her career concern her.

Will is also employed by a large company, but in his case it is a conglomerate consisting of a number of businesses all trading independently. Will's position is that of account executive – a job he has been doing since he joined the company. There is no career path mapped out for him and Will figures that unless he says something he will still be doing the same job in twenty years' time. As for promotion opportunities, they are there but, nine times out of ten, the positions that interest him go to outsiders.

Emma works for a company involved in environmental monitoring. The company employs five people including herself. Emma enjoys her job and gets on well with her bosses. She realizes, however, that she has little in the way of promotion prospects.

Here we have three people who face very different challenges with the realization of their ambitions and the extent to which assertiveness will be a factor in their success.

Sam can sit back and do nothing because the thinking is being done for her. Her only problem (if it arises) is if her ambitions change and if what she wants and what her employer has got pencilled in for her are no longer the same.

Will, on the other hand, is faced with the task of chiselling out his own career path in the fragmented organization where he works. He may find this proves to be an uphill struggle and the need to be assertive may figure highly in his list of considerations.

Emma is in a completely different situation. Assertiveness won't help her with the realization of her ambitions because the company she works for is too small. In short, she would be wasting her time making a case to her seniors. She would do better by putting her effort into searching the outside job market. She can decide for herself when the time is right for doing this.

Profiling

The case study of Sam, Will and Emma (case study 13) illustrates that, before putting your assertiveness to the test with the realization of career ambitions, you need first to make an assessment of your employer's capacity to deliver whatever it is that you are seeking (for example, a promotion). Failing to do so could lead you into situations where, irrespective of how assertive you are, you could be banging your head on a brick wall. For example:

- you want your boss's job, but your boss has no intention of moving on;
- you want a big pay rise, but your firm has just announced record losses;
- you are looking for a permanent job, but your firm only employs people on six-month contracts.

In all of the above situations, you are pursuing ambitions that, to all practical intents and purposes, are unattainable, and assertiveness won't make one jot of difference to the outcome.

Notepad

Making an assessment of your employer's capacity to deliver career ambitions is known as *profiling*. A more detailed examination of profiling is contained in another book in this series: *Teach Yourself Managing your own Career*.

Warning

Banging your head on brick walls is something you need to avoid. Apart from being painful, it carries the risk that you could go on doing so for years. The upshot? You fritter away a precious part of your life chasing career aspirations that are unattainable as far as your particular employer is concerned. Remember those precious years don't come round again. Remember too there are many more employers out there – employers who won't have the same constraints as the people you are working for currently.

Avoid value judgements

When profiling employers don't slip into the trap of branding them as 'good' or 'bad', because this obscures the real issues. All employers have limitations on what they can and can't deliver. Even in the case of Sam's multinational (case study 13), they may on the face of it look like the ideal career provider, but this only holds true up to the point where their plans for Sam's future and her own ideas match up. If, for example, Sam decides she wants to do something entirely different then she may find all kinds of shutters start to come up.

Moving ambitions forward

To sum up so far, we have been asking you to take a long hard look at your career ambitions to see:

- whether your ambitions are a true reflection of your talents (to see whether you are under- or overreaching);
- to what extent any under-reaching may be conditioned by lack of self-confidence and/or self-esteem.

Next we need to put the plan into action and see how well our assertiveness works for us when we put it to the test. Again let's use a case study to show one of the challenges we may face and at the same time to pull together some of the points we covered earlier.

Case study 14: Hans

Hans is an electrical engineer who works for a company that manufactures special purpose machinery for use in the printing industry. Hans has been doing this job for the last four years. He will be 28 in two months' time.

Hans's manager is Bill. Bill is 57 and recently took everyone by surprise by announcing he was going to take early retirement.

Straightaway it became apparent to Hans that this was his big chance. He'd always had the ambition to step into a management job one day but here – a little earlier than expected perhaps – was the ideal opportunity.

As a first step, Hans decided to bounce his ideas off Bill. He'd always got on well with Bill and trusted his judgement so, over a beer after work one night, he told Bill he was considering putting in an application. What did Bill think? Bill said he thought it was a good idea. After all there was no one else in the electrical engineering team who could be considered even remotely suitable. Bill warned, however that, Sol, the Engineering Director, might have a different opinion. Hans was only 27 after all and Sol could well take the view that he didn't have sufficient experience or depth of character to shoulder the responsibility of running one of the company's key technical areas.

Thanking Bill for being so candid, Hans went home and thought through his options. He saw Bill's point about not having enough experience (the same thought had occurred to him). In the end, however, he figured he'd got nothing to lose by applying for Bill's job so he decided to give it a whirl. Next morning he put his head round Sol's door and asked if he could spare him ten minutes later in the day.

The art of the possible

What we're seeing here is a young electrical engineer, Hans, presented with an opportunity to fulfil his ambition to get into a management job. He is concerned, however, that the opportunity has come up too soon and, because he lacks experience, he may be overreaching. A conversation with Bill, his boss, has confirmed this doubt although overall Bill is supportive of the view that Hans should be putting in an application. In other words, Hans has listened to the feedback and, although the messages are mixed, the feedback in the shape of Bill's comments is suggesting he should press on. Press on is what he decides to do.

What the case study shows is that the world of careers is not a nice tidy place where opportunities present themselves at exactly the right moment. In Hans's case, the 'right moment' would be in a few years' time when he has got more experience under his belt. However, opportunities don't come up every day, and seldom present themselves more than once.

When opportunities present themselves you've got to go for them, and this is what the art of the possible is all about. Let opportunities pass you by and you will be sorry. In Hans's case, he will probably find someone is recruited from outside to fill Bill's vacant slot and the avenue to promotion that's been opened up to him will be blocked off again and will probably remain so for many years to come. What this means for Hans is that if he wants to pursue his ambition to be a manager in his specialist field, he will probably have no option other than to try and find a suitable position with another employer. He may not want to do this of course.

Key point

Learn to be nimble on your feet and ready to take advantage of opportunities as and when they arise. Never procrastinate. Take the chances when they're there.

Communicate your ambitions

So, you have now done the groundwork and ensured, as far as you can, that:

- your ambitions are a fair and true reflection of your talents;
- your employers have the capacity to deliver what you are asking for.

The next step is to communicate your ambitions and here a reminder that failing to communicate ambitions is the main reason why so many people's aspirations get misread (a common cause for being passed by).

Prepare what you want to say

Here we go back to the lessons presented in Chapter 2, in particular:

- Don't say anything that will invite a negative response. Don't whine. Don't make threats.
- Focus on keeping the message concise. Remember the more you say, the easier it is for misunderstandings to creep in. Don't repeat yourself.
- Resist the urge to 'dress it up'. Speak plainly. Avoid meandering explanations. The only issue here is ensuring that your message gets across clearly.
- Don't try to sell yourself. Let the facts speak for themselves. For example, if you're good at your job and deserve to be promoted then everyone will be aware of the fact.

Identify contentious areas

Contentious means contentious to the person on the receiving end of your assertiveness and, since the subject is career ambitions, this will normally be your immediate boss. Here you're at an advantage because you know your boss and you know what he or she is likely to find contentious. In the case of Hans, he guessed that, in the eyes of Sol, the contentious part of his bid to step into Bill's shoes will be his lack of experience. What Hans needs to do therefore is to have some points ready just in case Sol brings his lack of experience up. What he could say, for example, is that whilst he may not have years of experience, he does have a track record with the company and he knows the product and the people (more than can be said for someone coming in from outside).

Handling meetings

You now know what you are going to say and how you are going to say it. The next step is to set up a meeting with your boss and, as with all meetings, your meeting needs to have an aim. The aim in this case is twofold:

- to communicate your ambition;
- to get a reaction.

As far as the meeting itself is concerned the following checklist of pointers may be helpful:

- Aim to bring the meeting to a close as soon as you can – don't protract the discussion any longer than necessary. Once you've said all that you need to say and you've got the boss's reaction then, from your point of view, the meeting is over.
- Don't get locked in arguments. If the boss is hostile to your ambitions then leave it at that. You are one step nearer to establishing that your ambition may not be attainable though you should always allow for the fact that the boss may be having a bad day. With this in mind an exit line like, 'Perhaps we both need to think things over' leaves the door open for the boss to have a change of heart. Remember to say thank you for listening.
- Don't expect immediate agreement. Your boss may end the discussion by saying something on the lines of, 'Leave it with me, I'll think it over'. Bear in mind also that this could be a coded message that the boss needs to run your ideas by someone higher up the ladder.

- Your boss may actually say that the decision on what you want is out of his or her remit and rests with higher authority. If this happens, find out whether you will have to make the running with the higher authority yourself or whether your boss will put forward your case for you. If the latter, see if you can get a reading on how sympathetic the boss is to your case.
- Where the ambition you're seeking to fulfil is within the boss's remit, you may get agreement there and then. In which case, end the discussion on this happy note and don't, as some experts would have you do, try to pin the boss down to time-scales. For example, if you've got the boss to agree to putting you in charge of the office, don't start pressing him/her for the effective date. There is a fine line between assertiveness and pushiness. The first is fine. The second inclines people to take up defensive postures. As to effective dates, we will be dealing with how to progress your ambitions shortly. As far as today is concerned, give yourself a pat on the back and leave it at that because you have achieved all that you set out to do.
- You may find the boss says something on the lines of, 'Yes, you're right to have these ambitions but you need more training/further education/experience before you have any chance of realizing them.' Treat comments like these as positive feedback and use them to fine-tune your ideas.

Warning

With this last point, saying you need more training/further education/experience may be a way of fobbing you off and the danger here is that you go away, get the training/further education/experience, then still find the doors are closed to you. In the end this boils down to a question of trust and any views you form need to be based on a wider appreciation of the boss's character over a range of issues.

How did it go?

In assessing the impact of your assertiveness, you need to take into account that some of your ambitions may not be realizable immediately. Having the boss say 'yes' seems like cast iron evidence that your assertiveness has worked and, in a case like that of Hans, where his ambition is one that will be realizable almost immediately, he can congratulate himself. Rather more difficult to deal with, however, are situations where the ambition, if it is realized at all, will be realized at some point in the future. How do you know whether the boss really meant it when he or she said 'yes'? For example, how do you guarantee that you will be tapped on the shoulder the next time the company wants to appoint an area manager?

The short answer to this question is that you can't and, let's face it, asking for firm promises wouldn't really have a lot of point (you could still get overlooked). However, what you need to go back to is the aim of your meeting. This, you will remember, was to communicate your ambition; to listen to the feedback.

In other words, the aim has been achieved. What you have done in fact is to try to program the boss into speaking to you the next time an area manager's job comes up. More importantly, however, you have delivered a tacit little warning that you won't be very happy if you get overlooked and slowly but surely, your silent bargaining power will start to bite. It will be evident to the boss that if the next area manager's job isn't offered to you then he or she runs the risk of seeing you leave.

Notepad

With ambitions that will come into fruition in the long term there is a clear need to monitor progress and to make sure that the commitment to you doesn't waver as time passes by. Monitoring progress is a subject we will be looking at shortly.

Failure

With career ambitions, assertiveness won't always work for you and occasionally you will run into a brick wall. Hans, for example, could find that Sol turns him down flat for Bill's job. How do you react to rejection?

On the face of it, being told 'no', 'never' or 'no way' seems like a completely negative event. However – and though it's sometimes hard to see – you have made progress, even if it's no more than being one step closer to realizing that your ambition isn't realizable with this particular employer.

Don't, whatever you do, let rejection become the cause of an argument over the fairness of the boss's verdict on you. Listen to what you're told, disengage and leave it at that. As we said earlier, there's always the possibility you caught the boss on a bad day and, once your silent bargaining power has started to work, you could find the boss comes back with a rather softer approach. The fact that you have not had a serious falling-out will make it easier for him or her to climb down.

Monitoring your progress

Where the ambition is one that you hope to realize at some point in the future, it is important that you monitor your progress to check that the force of your assertiveness doesn't dwindle with the passing of time (effectively, you get forgotten).

You could find that your meeting with the boss is followed by a long silence. The subject of your ambitions is never brought up again and, six or twelve months down the line, the progress you have made is zero. How do you deal with this? At what point do you read into these silences that the boss may be in need of another dose of assertiveness?

Silences have a number of possible explanations:

- Since the ambition is long-term it may be that there is nothing sinister about the lack of progress. It may be a case of 'no news is no news'.
- The boss has forgotten and, in this context, there is scope for genuine oversight with people who are constantly in the throes of dealing with conflicting pressures (today's typical senior manager).
- The boss doesn't have the authority (something that may not be apparent to you).
- The boss has been higher up the ladder and has been given a 'no'. Again he or she may have difficulty in telling you.
- The company's circumstances have changed – for example, something is going on that you may not be aware of and which has a bearing on the realization of your ambitions.

The list goes on but what is important with anything you do now is that you begin to form an opinion on whether your career ambitions are still on track.

What do you do? Simply rise to the challenge. Speak to the boss again and remember this is your career, your future, and any backing off won't serve your better interests. Be assertive – you've a right to be – and ask the boss (politely of course) if there is any progress to report on the direction you indicated you wanted to go in.

Set a time limit

Here, of course, you could simply run into a wall of prevarication. Mumbled excuses, promises to move your career concerns higher up the list of priorities, reassurances that everything will work out fine – we've all been there at one point or another. How do you deal with prevarication? A case study will help us to focus on the main issues. This is the experience Jane had when she asked for a rise which she felt she deserved.

Case study 15: Jane

Jane works for a vehicle rental company where she is employed as a manager in charge of a call centre which is effectively the hub of the company's business. Jane has been in this position for the last two years though her service with the company is longer (she spent four years on the front line taking calls).

Jane's big gripe is that her role in the company has never been recognized properly. She deals with 90 per cent of the hassle and effectively shields Josh, the owner, from the kind of confrontation with customers he would find painful. In return she is paid a salary which she views as a pittance and which takes no account of the long hours she works.

One night, when the phones have gone quiet, Jane decides the time has come to have a few words with Josh and, seeing him alone in his office, she puts her head round the door and asks to see him.

Remembering to stay positive and say how much she enjoys her job and working for the company, Jane makes her case for why her salary should be increased. Josh listens attentively but, when she finishes speaking, he makes no comment other than to say he'll think over what she's had to say and get back to her. Not knowing what to make of this, Jane thanks him for sparing her the time and goes back to her office.

Six weeks pass during which time Jane has daily contact with Josh on a whole range of issues. The subject of her pay isn't raised, however, and Jane starts to form the view that Josh may have conveniently 'forgotten'. Pleasant character that he is, Josh has the reputation of being tightfisted particularly when it comes to salaries.

Steeling herself, Jane goes in to see Josh again to remind him about their previous conversation and to ask him if he has now had a chance to consider the case she put to him for an increase in her pay. Smiling, Josh reassures her that the matter hasn't slipped his mind. He needs to speak to his accountant, he explains, and his accountant has been away on holiday.

Thinking it over later, Jane isn't sure again what to make of this. Six weeks is a long time for anybody to be on holiday and, though she is still inclined to believe Josh, there is doubt in her mind that he may be stringing her along.

A further two months pass by during which time Josh is out of the office more than usual (a rival business is up for sale and Josh is interested in buying it). Finally Jane manages to catch him as he pops into the office early one evening to pick up some papers. Has he been able to speak to his accountant yet? she asks him. Apologizing for not getting back to her, Josh replies that he has but his accountant is currently looking at budgets and, until that exercise is completed, he won't know how much money is available for paying salary increases. When will Josh be in a position to give her an answer? Josh says it's hard to say because, with the purchase of the rival business pending, there are a number of conflicting demands on the accountant's time.

Two more months go by with still no news from Josh. The purchase of the rival business goes through and, with Josh heavily involved, his visits to the office have become less and less frequent. For her part Jane is still not sure what to think. It could be that Josh is still waiting for the figures from his accountant. On the other hand he could be dodging the issue and hoping she won't raise it again.

The points to pick out from this case study are as follows:

- Jane has used her assertiveness and made the case for the salary increase she thinks she deserves.
- Her boss's reaction is difficult to read.
- Attempts to draw him (more assertiveness) haven't worked.
- She isn't sure what to do next.

We could guess all day at the reasons why Jane's boss has chosen to prevaricate on the question of her pay rise. We could be looking at a case of someone who is habitually careful with his money or it could that Josh's new acquisition has left him stretched for cash and struggling to keep on top of costs – who knows? All that matters at the end of the day is that Jane is still no nearer to knowing whether she is going to get her pay rise or not than she was at the outset. How does she deal with this situation? What do you do when you can't get a straight answer from your boss, or where a perfectly legitimate ambition you're seeking to pursue never seems to materialize?

The answer here is to be assertive and to take charge of the situation. What's a reasonable period of time for your employer to come up with what you're looking for? The answer, of course, depends on the magnitude of your ambitions. A pay rise, for example, would be more or less immediate, whereas a seat on the board of directors may be some time in the future. Whatever the ambition, put a time limit on how long it will take to achieve – two months, two years, before you're 40 – the point being that, if your employer doesn't deliver before the expiry of the time limit, you put the ambition in the category of ambitions that aren't realizable in the context of your current employment. You move on and you don't allow yourself to be messed round any further.

Warning

You can squander away the best years of your life waiting for empty promises to materialize. You need to keep it in mind that those best years don't come round again.

Watch for bad signs

When it comes to the business of progressing career ambitions, bosses who procrastinate or try to fob you off with excuses are a bad sign. A rather more obvious bad sign is where you are looking for promotion and you see someone being brought in from outside to do the job that you would like to do. Your boss (employer) knows about your ambitions so there can be no misunderstandings – you really have been passed by! This is really the signal to stand by to get on your bike.

Triggering the leverage

Being assertive and making your career ambitions known to people who matter is designed to bring pressure to bear on them, or trigger leverage. The same people are going to fathom pretty quickly that, if you don't get what you want, you will start to get restless meaning you might decide to go off and invest your talents somewhere else. How well this leverage works depends entirely on the store of silent bargaining power you have built up and this is a point we have drawn your attention to a number of times already in this book. If the leverage triggers then it's usually down to your silent bargaining power and vice versa.

Shaping the future

Assertiveness in career management is about:

- making your career ambitions known to the people who matter (people who can influence the outcomes for you);
- ensuring your ambitions are met.

What is also important, however, is that you see this application of assertiveness as a *continuous process* rather than a single event. How do you do this?

Continuous adding value to yourself

In progressing career ambitions we have seen the link between assertiveness and silent bargaining power and its importance. Assertiveness is the transmitting force for silent bargaining power. What's more, silent bargaining and assertiveness are interdependent. One without the other is largely useless. Someone who has built up a lot of worth with their employer won't get the pay-off they deserve unless their employer is made aware of the directions they want to move in.

The further point to silent bargaining power is that it is *acquirable*. For example:

- You can extend your skills base.
- You can add to your qualifications.
- You can widen your experience.
- You can put more effort into your work.
- You can seek to improve your image.

All of the above will serve to add value in the eyes of your employer. It will give your assertiveness something tangible to back it up. It will make your assertiveness perform for you.

Get everyone used to you being ambitious

Whilst some people don't have a problem telling the world they're ambitious, others fight shy because they associate being ambitious with being pushy and/or self-proclaiming.

There is a big difference between:

- ambitions that are held legitimately and that are a true reflection of your talents; and
- ambitions that are based on nothing other than an inflated opinion of yourself.

With the former, everyone will take you seriously (you have silent bargaining power), whereas with the latter, your assertiveness will be viewed as a laughing matter and will put a dent in your credibility.

Having identified the ambitions you're right to have, then you need to get used to sharing your thoughts with people who count – people like your boss. What emerges from this ongoing appreciation of where you're coming from in life is a constant awareness of your silent bargaining power. For example, if you make it known that you want to be the next area manager and the topic becomes a talking point then there are no big surprises when you put in for the next vacancy that comes up. Indeed you may find that there is no need to say anything because your boss approaches you first (cast-iron proof that your silent bargaining power and assertiveness have worked).

Questions and answers

Dealing with negative feedback

Q *At a recent appraisal interview I was told by my boss that she didn't consider me suitable for a team leader's position. Since this is my ambition, how am I supposed to deal with this feedback? Should I be saying something back to her?*

A Did your boss say *why* she considered you unsuitable? For example, did she say you lacked experience and/or qualifications? In which case the signal to you is to act on the feedback and figure out ways in which you could get the experience and/or qualifications. This should include you putting pressure on your boss to provide training. Short of this, view negative feedback of this kind for what it's worth which, at the end of the day, is one person's view of another. Even though it may seem pretty damning, take heart because there are plenty of instances of people who've been given the put-down by one boss and then gone on to work for someone else with a completely different attitude. Also, allow for the fact that the boss may have been having a bad day. Case study 1 (Jenny) has echoes of your situation.

Ambitions curtailed by fear

Q *I work for a company in the construction industry where there is little or no investment in training and where, as a consequence, I am underachieving. I know I should be looking for a job somewhere else but I am put off by the fact that the construction industry is notoriously volatile and, if I move to a new employer, I will be in the position of last in, top of the list if the need for redundancies arises. In contrast I've chalked up nearly 15 years' service with my present employer, meaning at least I've got reasonable job security. Part of my concern is that I'm the main bread winner in a family of four and I have a mortgage to pay. Am I right to be playing safe?*

A The meaning of the word 'safe' is relative, and in some ways, playing safe is one of the most dangerous things you can do. However, first of all you need to do a proper risk assessment of the upsides and downsides attached to changing jobs. The upside, it would seem, is the realization of your ambition (better position, better pay, better prospects, etc.), whereas the downside is the catastrophe that would descend on you if for some reason it all went wrong (the financial fallout from finding yourself umemployed). However, consider the risks attached to staying where you are. The upside in this case is sticking with the devil you know and the relative security. The downside is continuing to underachieve with the knock-on effect this will have not just on your earnings capacity but also on your confidence and self-esteem.

Turning down a promotion

Q *After 18 months of waiting I finally got the promotion I was looking for (a seat on the board of management). Imagine, however, my disappointment when I discovered that the promotion wasn't accompanied by any increase in pay. Should I turn down the promotion? Is this the best way of using my assertiveness?*

A No it isn't and, in the absence of any explanation, perhaps you need to take into account that your company may be looking for evidence of your ability to perform in your new capacity before conferring extra pay on you. Our advice? Give the new job your best shot then if there is no movement with your salary within, say, six months have a go at putting forward a case. Remember that with six months' satisfactory job performance to your credit you will have more in the way of silent bargaining power to back you up.

Being walked over

Q *Not complaining sounds to me like a guaranteed way of getting walked over. How do you square this with being more assertive?*

A You miss the point. Complaining and whining will only serve to put people's backs up and invite a negative response. The discussion that's supposed to be about your career ambitions will probably get side-tracked into an argument about whether your assertions are right or not. The result? You achieve nothing and you aren't seeing eye to eye with your bosses any more.

Summary

This chapter has explored the part played by assertiveness in career management – notably the part played in putting together properly defined ambitions and transmitting silent bargaining power to the point where it will exert leverage. In particular, we have laid emphasis on the importance of all the links in the chain:

- having ambitions that are a true reflection of your talents;
- using assertiveness to communicate those ambitions to the people who matter;
- adding value and accumulating silent bargaining power;
- bringing silent bargaining power to bear;
- monitoring the result.

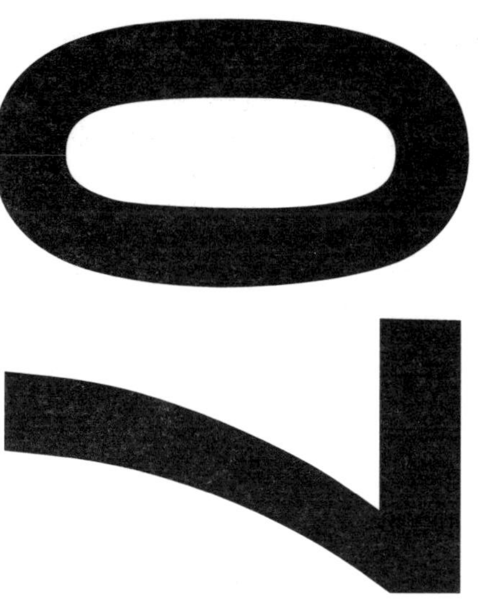

assertiveness in job applications

In this chapter you will learn:

- **how to get what you want out of the job market**
- **how to make employers understand you**
- **how assertiveness will help you to be successful in interviews**

Defining your aims

This is important. Embarking on job applications with no clear set of aims is asking for trouble. The next case study demonstrates some of the problems:

Case study 16: Rachel

Rachel works in sales for a health sector company. She has been doing this job for the last four years.

Rachel has decided the time has come to make a move. Her last two pay rises haven't been brilliant and, just recently, some new reporting procedures have been put in place that aren't to Rachel's liking.

Rachel's first step is to dig out her CV. She last used her CV when she applied for her present position and she is pleased she remembered to save it onto a disk. She is even more pleased to find that her CV is only in need of a few minor tinkerings to bring it up-to-date. Her present position needs to be added onto her employment history and her address and telephone number have changed.

Over the next few weeks Rachel makes a point of scanning the job ads in the local evening newspaper and applying for any interesting looking sales positions that catch her eye. In most cases this involves sending off her CV with an accompanying letter. As a result of this activity she gets invited to attend three interviews. Here, however, she runs into a problem. She has used up all her holiday entitlement and this leaves her with no alternative other than to make up three separate excuses for taking time off work. In two cases she is asked to go back for second interviews meaning yet more excuses and all the time she can see that the Sales Director is getting more and more suspicious to the point where he is starting to ask awkward questions.

At last Rachel gets offered one of the positions. It is with a small manufacturing company seeking to recruit someone to develop sales of a new product and, since the main buyers will be hospitals and health authorities, Rachel's background is ideal. However, the crunch comes when Rachel is told about the salary. It is little advance on what she is currently earning and, in her view, it hardly justifies making the move. Will the company improve its offer?

The answer Rachel gets back is no. The salary represents the maximum they can go to and, in any case, they feel it's up to Rachel to prove herself by bringing in orders before they consider paying her more.

The upshot is Rachel decides to turn the offer down. What bothers her now though is that she will have to go back to square one with her job applications. As to having more time off work to attend interviews, she is seriously concerned that the Sales Director will be demanding to know what's going on.

So what's going wrong for Rachel? The points to pick out from the case study are as follows:

- Rachel's motive for putting herself on the job market is not very clear. She has an issue with her salary and she doesn't like the new reporting systems – in other words she appears to be driven by *negative* forces (grudges and grouses).
- There is no evidence that Rachel has thought through where she sees her next move taking her. The need to see a significant improvement in her salary (sufficient to make the move worthwhile) only appears to have entered into her thinking at the point where a job offer was put in her hands.
- Certainly she didn't include her aspirations and ambitions in her updated CV.
- As a consequence of this the mismatch between Rachel's salary aspirations and what the company who sought to employ her could afford to pay her did not become apparent until the very end of the selection process. This is the difficulty of applying for jobs where no salary is quoted.
- Everyone's time was wasted – notably Rachel's.
- Rachel is in her boss's bad books.
- The experience she has had is disappointing

Dangers of not having any clearly defined aims

The lessons to be drawn from Rachel's case study can be put under two headings:

- **Time-wasting** Unless you're lucky enough to work in a job where your movements aren't subject to too much scrutiny, the time you can have off work to go to interviews without inviting the suspicion of your bosses is always limited. Therefore any time you spend on going for jobs that wouldn't interest you even if they were offered to you must be seen as a waste of one of your most precious resources.

- **Discouragement** Putting a lot of effort into making an application and then finding, like Rachel did, that the job doesn't come up to scratch is disappointing to say the least. However, if you keep repeating the experience, you will find the cumulative effect is a downward spiral, which in turn leads to despair, and you may well end up giving up because you feel you're not getting anywhere.

Warning

Two of the most common reasons why people give up with their job applications prematurely are because (a) they find it difficult to take more time off work to go to interviews and (b) because they feel discouraged because they feel they're not getting anywhere. Because of this they never get to see the true extent of the market for their talents. They fail to connect with the best opportunities available to them and, as a result, they underachieve.

Job applications and assertiveness

Assertiveness is about being in control of your life and, applied to job applications, this means making sure they have a proper sense of purpose and direction – one that you determine at the outset and one that is consistent with what you want to achieve in the next stage of your career.

In Rachel's case, you remember, the direction was there but it was driven by *negative* forces:

- dissatisfaction with her pay;
- a grouse over new reporting procedures.

Nowhere did we see evidence to suggest she had sat down and thought through a clear set of aims – *positive* statements about the direction in which she wanted to see her job applications taking her.

Key point

Step one in bringing greater assertiveness into your job applications is to forget your grudges and grouses in your current job and turn your attention to the gains you expect to make by changing jobs. Supplant negative thoughts with positive ones, and do this in advance of venturing out into the job market. In this way you will avoid time-wasting and the resulting discouragement.

Targeting

Targeting is the business of defining aims against a set of benchmarks – being clear in your mind what you expect from your next job move prior to putting yourself on the market. Targeting is a simple exercise and you can do it by going through the following checklist:

Targeting checklist

- **The job** Are you looking for the next job up the ladder, for example, or would a sideways step suffice because your current job isn't very safe? Alternatively, are you seeking to break into an entirely new field – a complete change of career?
- **The pay** What are you expecting to earn in your next job? Is, for example, salary the only reason you're seeking to make a move? In which case, the advancement has got to be big enough to make the move worthwhile .
- **The hours** Are you looking for a job with normal nine-to-five hours or do other commitments mean you can only work part-time? If you are in an occupation where shift work and/or unsociable hours are sometimes a requirement, how would you view these?
- **The organization** Are you looking to work in any particular industry, profession or field of commercial activity? Also under this heading come considerations such as the size and culture of the organization you would like to work for.
- **The prospects** Are prospects important to you? If so it could be better to focus your attention on larger employers or those in high-growth situations?
- **The training** Are you seeking to become qualified – in which case, is it important to you that your next employer is able to provide you with training?

- **The area** Are you looking for a job within commuting distance of where you live now or are you prepared to work elsewhere?
- **The risk** Is job security a major item for you or would you be prepared to consider something with a little more risk attached to it, for example a start-up business?
- **Anything else** By this we mean anything else that's important to you. For example, do you have a medical problem that could make it difficult for you to work in certain situations or environments?

Reasons for targeting

Targeting is about being selective. It has two aims:

- cutting down on failure (discouragement);
- cutting down on time-wasting.

In Rachel's case, if she had done her targeting properly she would only be applying for jobs with employers who could afford to pay her the salary she is seeking.

Engaging with reality

All well and good, we can hear you saying, but what if Rachel's ideas on salary were over the top? What if the figure she set her sights on was over and above the market rate for someone with her skills, experience and qualifications?

What is important (always) is to ensure that what you're looking for in a new job and what the market has to offer line up – in other words that, in your efforts to be more assertive, you're not setting off on a quest for a job that doesn't exist or only comes up very occasionally. The problem for you, of course, is that at this stage you won't have too much idea what the market for your talents has to offer. You won't know whether your pay aspirations are too high or whether the market would view you as inexperienced or underqualified. How do you get round this one?

- **Check the job ads:** You'll be doing this anyway, but see how many jobs match your targeting benchmarks and, most importantly, see whether you are qualified to do these jobs (be honest with yourself).

- **Talk to recruitment consultants:** Though the standards of recruitment consultants (agencies) are not always very consistent, they should at least be able to give you an opinion on whether you are being realistic. Recruitment consultants who specialize in people like you should be the best informed.
- **Tap into your networks:** Is there anyone among your circle of contacts who has experience of shopping the job market recently. If so, do they have any useful advice they can pass on to you on what's available 'out there'?

From these three sources you should be able to form an appreciation of whether your targeting is engaging with reality or not.

Feedback and flexibility

Targeting benchmarks should never be viewed as cast in stone. As you get more and more experience of the niche market for people like you, new ideas will start to develop and you should allow this to happen. In particular, keep your ears open to pick up any feedback you get from:

- employers (for example, at job interviews);
- consultants;
- people like employment advisers and outplacement counsellors.

Incorporating feedback into your ideas will strengthen them. You could, for example, decide that, in the light of the feedback you've received, your pay aspirations are too high – in which case you could bring them down a notch or two. Alternatively you could decide you're not so badly paid after all.

Warning

Be wary of feedback from a single source. The person delivering the feedback may not be well informed or may be expressing a highly personal and potentially prejudiced opinion. Therefore, take it with a pinch of salt if your employer pours scorn on one of your cherished ideas, but take more note if you hear the same criticism from more than one source. The signal to you then could be to reflect on what you're doing and perhaps think again.

Communicating your aims

The next step in bringing more assertiveness into your job applications is to make everyone aware of where you are coming from and what you are seeking to achieve. How do you do this?

Your CV

Rachel (case study 16), you remember, spent some time bringing her CV up-to-date. What she omitted to do, however, was to include in her CV any mention of what she was hoping to gain by moving jobs – in her case, to gain an improvement in her pay. Had she thought to include this information, the mismatch between what she was looking for and what the small manufacturing company could afford to pay would have become apparent at the outset. More to the point, with her salary aspirations set out clearly in her CV it would be reasonably safe to assume that if she did get asked to attend any interviews it would be for jobs with employers who were able to meet her aspirations.

Key point

A common mistake is to see your CV as there to get you interviews. Whilst this is important, it is equally important that your CV conveys enough about you and your ambitions to enable employers to spot any mismatches between what you want and what they've got to offer. They will be as keen to avoid the time-wasting as you are.

Where do you put this information about what you are seeking to achieve by moving jobs? If it doesn't have one already, your CV needs to contain a section headed 'Ambitions' or something similar – somewhere where you can list out your targeting benchmarks, for example, 'I'm looking for a job in sales with fresh challenges and where I can hope to earn a salary in excess of £xxx per annum.'

Notepad

As Rachel (case study 16) found, a difficulty all job seekers face is the advertisement in the press or on a website that doesn't give any information on salary beyond the usual jumble of words such as 'negotiable', 'attractive' 'commensurate with the responsibilities', etc. The job looks worth pursuing but, without any insight into the pay, how do you know whether it's worth applying for or not?

Here the sensible approach would seem to be to ring up and ask for details of the salary over the phone – on the pretext that you don't want to waste anyone's time. Sensible it may be, but sadly the evidence of this approach actually working is rather thin on the ground. Employers have reasons for being cagey about pay and their caginess usually extends to how they deal with casual callers. In short, the answer you get may not move you forward very far.

So how do you deal with advertisements without salaries?

- Follow the advice so far in this chapter and revisit your CV.
- Satisfy yourself that no one reading it would get any wrong ideas about your pay aspirations.
- Send off your application and see what happens.

If you get a 'sorry but no thank you' letter (or no reply at all), the chances are that what the employer can afford to pay falls short of the figure you've flagged up in your CV. Note in passing that rejection in these circumstances is nothing to get wound up about. Instead, you should be giving yourself a pat on the back for avoiding a potentially time-wasting and painful experience.

Application forms

Where you're asked to fill in an application form as part of a selection process, this gives you yet another opportunity to bring your assertiveness to bear.

Application forms follow no standard patterns, but many contain a question along the lines of, 'Why are you applying for this job?' This is where you can list what you're expecting your next job to provide, in the same way that you've done in your CV. Again, employers are given the opportunity to compare what they have to offer with what you are looking for and to identify any possible mismatches.

Two points to bear in mind about application forms are:

- Employers actually read them, whereas CVs tend to get a quick flick through and some vital aspect of your aspirations may be missed.
- Application forms frequently set the agenda for interviews (when you attend an interview notice how often the interviewer has your application form on the desk).

Telephone vetting

Due to pressures on time, employers are becoming increasingly selective about who they ask in for an interview and one of the knock-on effects of this has been the greater use of pre-interview telephone vetting. This is usually done by a quick phone call, the aim of which is to establish your general suitability.

At some point during one of these phone calls an opportunity usually presents itself to trot out your targeting benchmarks – a question about why you're applying for the job, for example.

Interviews

Given that in the stages leading up to an interview your motives for putting yourself on the job market have been made crystal clear to everyone, it seems safe enough to assume that an invitation to attend an interview is a signal that what you're looking for and what the employer has to offer are broadly in line. Assertiveness and job interviews is a subject we will be looking at shortly, but suffice it to say at this stage that one of your main tasks at an interview is to carry your assertiveness forward and not to let it wither when it comes to dealing with an employer face-to-face.

Recruitment consultants

As part of your job hunting strategy you may decide to register with a firm of recruitment consultants (or an employment agency). Some of these firms of consultants are Internet-based so registering could involve giving your details on-line.

What is of crucial importance with recruitment consultants is that they *understand* fully what it is you want them to do for you, and what opportunities will interest you and what won't.

Dealing with recruitment consultants can sometimes be painful, as they are driven by the need to get results both for themselves and for the clients they serve. In part this need is fuelled by the fact that many of them are paid on commission. Unfortunately, focusing on commission earnings can sometimes lead to recruitment consultants phoning you up with all sorts of opportunities, most of which won't interest you in the slightest.

How can assertiveness help you?

- Don't feel apologetic towards recruitment consultants who bombard you with every job opportunity that comes on their books and don't be afraid to say no.
- Remind the consultant of the original brief you gave them and point out the way in which the opportunity under discussion falls short.
- Hear warning bells if the consultant suggests to you that you are trying to be too picky and choosy. Don't succumb to this kind of pressure. If you're going to modify your targeting benchmarks do it in the light of experience rather than random comments from someone who may be working to a different agenda.
- Go through your targeting benchmarks again. Ask the consultant if he/she is now clear.
- If you don't think the consultant is being selective in what he/she offers you, find another firm of consultants to register with.

Recruitment consultants are a good source of job opportunities and an important means of access to the important invisible market (the jobs that aren't advertised). This is why it is worth putting some time and effort into briefing them properly and keeping them on course. In doing this try to understand where they're coming from too. Most importantly, don't come across as awkward or impossible to please because this will put them off wanting to talk to you.

Networking

Networking your way into jobs means putting the feelers around your circle of contacts and seeing what there is for you out there. Networking is the way into jobs:

- which haven't been advertised (the invisible market again);
- where there is little or no competition;
- where sometimes a position is created specially for you and on the strength of what your contact knows about you.

How will a more assertive approach help you when it comes to networking your way into jobs? The next case study explores this question:

Case study 17: Seb and Anthony

Seb is a design engineer who works for a company who manufacture machinery for the food processing and packaging industry. Seb's company have been going through hard times recently, culminating in an announcement by the Managing Director that there will be no pay increases at the end of the year and, worse still, no overtime until further notice. This news leaves Seb feeling gutted. His wife, Zoe, is expecting a baby in February and the two of them had plans to move from their flat into a three-bedroom house. The money Seb earns from working overtime figured prominently in these plans but, with the overtime gone, Seb realizes they will have to put the plans on hold.

Seb is friends with Anthony. Anthony and he did their training with the same company, but now Anthony works for a small design engineering consultancy where he earns good money. Seb meets Anthony one evening for a drink. Inevitably the subject of pay comes up and Seb tells Anthony about the loss of his overtime and how this will affect the plans he and Zoe had made to move to a bigger house. Seb adds that because of this he is thinking of looking for another job.

The next day, Anthony is talking to his boss, Ray, who is the founder and sole owner of the design consultancy. He mentions Seb and the fact he is on the market for a better-paid job and Ray immediately pricks up his ears. There could well be a slot in the team for another experienced design engineer, Ray explains, and asks Anthony to fix up an interview.

Seb is slightly taken aback by Anthony's call. On the one hand he is appreciative that Anthony has put out the feelers for him but, on the other, he realizes he hasn't really thought through all the ramifications of leaving his job. He agrees to the interview, but already a number of doubts are beginning to creep into his mind.

The interview turns out to be a very informal affair at the end of which Ray offers Seb a job on a much higher salary than the one he is earning currently. What bothers Seb though is that in a consultancy he will be expected to work on a wider range of projects than he does now including some that will be outside his field of experience. He mentions this point to Ray. Ray, however, is dismissive saying that Seb will soon get the hang of things.

Agreeing to think over Ray's offer and get back to him by the end of the week, Seb leaves the interview with his mind in turmoil. The offer looks good and, yes, the extra money would enable Zoe and him to put their plan to move up the housing market into action. He is seriously concerned, however, that, once in the consultancy, there would be considerable pressure on him to perform. The snag then would be if, for any reason, he didn't come up to scratch. Seb's reading of Ray is that he wouldn't be the kind of boss to hold back if it came to giving an employee the short, sharp exit treatment. Seb sees at once that he is now in a tricky position. If he turns Ray's offer down, he could be causing difficulties for Anthony who put in a good word for him. Not unreasonably, Ray is going to feel his time has been wasted and Anthony could get the blame.

What are the lessons here?

- Don't use your network contacts as sounding boards for your gripes and groans. When it comes to jobs, it gives the impression that you're being driven solely by negative forces and anything will do.
- Remember the importance of being assertive when it comes to feeding out messages to network contacts. If you want them to help you find another job, then it pays to make this crystal clear and leave them in no doubt.
- Make sure the messages you feed out are *complete* messages.
- Always make clear to your contacts exactly what you want them to do for you. Don't leave any room for guesswork or improvisation when it comes to deciding what's best for you.
- Set the parameters by telling your contacts how far you want them to go and at what point you want them to stop and report back. For instance, you may want to know more about the job before you commit yourself to an interview.

Key point

Assertiveness enables you to control networks and make them perform effectively for you. Given this control you should be able to avoid no-win situations of the kind that Seb found himself in. Note that assertiveness in professional networking is the subject of Chapter 8.

Assertiveness and job interviews

There are a number of common misunderstandings about assertiveness and job interviews and, to help expose some of these misunderstandings, let's use another case study.

Case study 18: Emily

Emily is a Management Accountant and she is attending a preliminary interview for a position with a large hotel and leisure chain. Her interview is with the Human Resources Manager, John.

When she arrives just before her appointed time, Emily is told the interviews are running 20 minutes late. She is asked to take a seat in reception and, while she is waiting, another candidate arrives.

When she is finally shown into John's office, he apologizes for the delay, explaining that a candidate for an interview earlier in the day arrived late due to a hold-up on the motorway. He then starts to go through Emily's application form, but Emily, keen to practise her assertiveness skills, asks it if would be easier if she told him a bit about herself. John seems uncertain at first and hesitates before he says yes, whereupon Emily embarks on a detailed oral version of her CV that she has spent the last few days rehearsing.

Ten minutes into this presentation, John interrupts her saying he needs to move on because he has got other candidates to see. Emily is taken aback by this – partly because she is only halfway through her presentation, and partly because she purposely left the most relevant parts of her experience to the end to act as a kind of grand finale. She tries to explain this to John but in vain because he is already firing questions at her. His pace from hereon is brisk to say the least and, on two occasions, he actually cuts her answers short. At the end he asks her if she wants to ask any questions, but by now Emily is too perplexed to think of anything. He closes off by thanking her for attending the interview and promises to get back to her.

A week later Emily gets a letter to say she hasn't been successful. She blames this outcome on a bad interview with a bad interviewer – someone who didn't give her the chance to bring out her best points.

This is an example of interviewee and interviewer with totally different agendas. The interviewee (Emily) is too focused on delivering her prepared presentation to be aware that the interviewer (John) is running late with his interviews and struggling hard to catch up. The case study illustrates how planning for interviews can actually go against you if you plan anything which isn't concise, flexible and capable of being adapted to the circumstances.

Identifying your strong points

This is where assertiveness with job interviews starts. Ask yourself what it is about you that employers are going to find most interesting. Is it, for example, your experience? Or, is it the fact that you can converse fluently in five European languages? Strong points are the attributes you have which match up with the requirements of the job.

Warning

Take care that what you may identify as a strong point may not be seen in the same way by the interviewer. For example, you may view the ten years' experience you had running a large ship repair yard in the Far East as brilliant stuff, whereas an employer looking for a manager for a small software business probably wouldn't see it as being too relevant. The message? Strong points are strong points for a particular job. In other words, from application to application, your strong points should differ.

Weak areas

Just as important as your strong points are the weak areas in your application and identifying where they are. A weak area could be, for example, that you don't have a particular qualification that an employer has listed as desirable or preferable. A central part of your planning for interviews is deciding how you are going to deal with weak areas if they should come up. For example, do you have plans to get the qualification in question? Or do you feel you have other qualifications which are just as important?

Key point

What's important about interviews is *controlling the messages* you feed out about yourself and making sure in particular that any strong points you have are emphasized. Emily, you remember, failed in this respect. Her strong points (her relevant experience) were tucked into the end part of her presentation – the part that didn't get delivered because she ran out of time.

Interview questions and answers

There is a natural tendency for candidates' strong points to come out in interviews. Interviewers focus on aspects of candidates' backgrounds and experience that interest them, and controlling the messages is simply a case of answering the questions. Being assertive and trying to take the interview over (as Emily did) should not be necessary.

Questions interviewers don't ask

The biggest danger with interviews (and where assertiveness will help you) is where:

- interviews aren't given enough time;
- the interviewer is poor or inexperienced.

Notepad

Some interviews do not go well and the candidates concerned are justified in feeling short-changed. Just about everyone who has been active on the job market in recent years will have chalked up at least one bad interview experience.

Interviews that run out of time

If you sense, like Emily did, that the interview is going to close before you've had chance to bring in one or more of your strong points, then this is the time to hit the emergency button. Say something along the lines of, 'Oh by the way I noticed in your ad that you use ZZZ software. If you look at my CV you'll see I used ZZZ in my last job. I worked with it for about three and a half years.'

Warning

CVs are used to select candidates for interviews and, where there are large numbers of candidates, the time given to reading each one may not be very great. This is why you should never assume that some cherished piece of information you've put in your CV will automatically be picked up when it comes to the final selection stages for a job. Your CV may be given a second viewing, but the people making the final selection decision may be relying more on documents such as application forms and interview notes. If you feel you have a strong point that will work in your favour, make sure it gets a mention at the interview. Keep hammering it home.

Incomplete information

Inexperienced interviewers, or those pushed for time, sometimes omit to ask all they need to ask. They get half the story and then they move on. Consider the next scenario. The candidate is being interviewed for a job as a production engineer where one of the requirements is to be able to use YYY software. The requirement wasn't mentioned in the advertisement for the job so the candidate isn't aware of it.

Interviewer: I want to come onto your programming skills. You have been with Oddjobs Engineering for nearly three years. What software have you been using?

Candidate: Mainly ZZZ.

Interviewer: What about YYY?

Candidate: Not a lot. We've recently purchased a machining centre with YYY controls but I've not been involved with it very much.

....

Interviewer: What about the position you held previously with Whizzround Turned Parts?

Candidate: That was YYY. I worked with it continuously for eight years.

The significance of the dotted line in the script is that this is where some interviewers would have terminated the interrogation. As a result, the view they would have formed quite incorrectly was that the candidate didn't have a lot of knowledge of YYY systems, and the candidate's chances of being offered the job would have been reduced.

The lesson here is to try and spot what's behind the question and, using your assertiveness skills, make sure that the interviewer gets the full picture. In the example above, this could mean jumping in if the interviewer attempts to move on before the full picture is revealed.

Assertiveness and job offers

For many people, the worrying starts when they get offered a job. Should they accept it or turn it down? Let's see how assertiveness can help when it comes to making this decision.

Cold feet

Applying for jobs can be great therapy. If your boss is giving you a hard time or if you didn't get the pay rise you expected, writing off for a few jobs will immediately make you feel better. You discover there are other options open to you and the world is suddenly a bigger and more exciting place.

The buzz that goes with making applications continues through to the interview stage. You find your confidence growing, and being picked for a shortlist really puts a spring in your stride.

But then you get offered the job and suddenly it's make your mind up time. Things aren't quite so simple any more. How seriously have you considered leaving (really)? How do you feel about saying goodbye to old friends and familiar places and taking the long lonely walk into the unknown?

It is at this point that many candidates start to develop cold feet. They end up turning down perfectly good offers simply because they don't have the confidence to say yes.

Weighing up offers

There is a distinction, however, between having cold feet for no reason and having cold feet because there's something about the offer that isn't to your liking – where you see turning the offer down as being the sensible thing to do. Let's see what happened to Gus in the next case study:

Case study 19: Gus

Gus is a Projects Manager and he has been offered a job by a large multinational company with a good salary and perks package. The problem, however, is that when he gets confirmation of the offer in writing, it comes with a voluminous set of staff conditions and, included in the small print of these conditions, is a clause stating that all management personnel are engaged on the basis that they are prepared to relocate to any part of the world as and when the need should arise. Gus's concerns are twofold:

- There was no mention of the condition at any of the interviews.
- He is a family man with a wife in a career job and two children who are doing well in local schools – relocating at short notice to some far flung part of the globe is the very last thing he would want to do.

So what's Gus to make of this?

- Has there been a mistake at the company's end? (Has he been sent the wrong set of conditions?)
- Or are they trying to pull the wool over his eyes?

The difficulty for Gus, of course, is that he is dealing with people he doesn't know. How should he proceed? One option open to Gus is to turn the offer down. Let's go back to the case study, however, and find out what he actually did.

Case study 19 (continued): Gus

The next day, Gus puts in a call to the person who offered him the job (the Projects Director) and points out:

- the discrepancy between the written conditions and what was said at the interview;
- his situation (his family circumstances and why relocation would be out of the question for him).

The Projects Director says he's aware of the compulsory relocation clause in the standard conditions of employment but, as it's hardly ever invoked, he felt it wasn't worth mentioning at the interview. Certainly in Gus's case it wouldn't be a problem because relocation is only ever an issue with operational grades. 'Can this be put into writing?' Gus asks. The Projects Director says he can't see why not.

By being assertive Gus has renegotiated a term in his offer of employment which was not to his liking. In this case, the offer was a perfectly good one so turning it down would have been a pity.

Notepad

Contrary to what most people think, a candidate in receipt of a job offer is usually in a very strong position when it comes to re-negotiating terms. True, the employer can say 'no', but in doing so they run the risk of the candidate turning the offer down. This would then put them in one of two positions:

- having to offer the job to their second choice (never a very inviting prospect);
- having to go back to square one and start the recruitment process all over again (even less inviting).

Enticement

Assertiveness and staying in control also mean knowing when to say 'no'. This isn't always easy, as the next case study demonstrates:

Case study 20: Frank

Frank is a Sales Manager in the plastics industry. He has a good reputation for attracting business, especially in the automotive sector where he has built up a large number of contacts. Two months ago, Frank received an approach out of the blue from a competitor. They offered him a job on a vastly improved salary together with a top-of-the-range company car.

Taken by surprise, Frank didn't know what to do about the offer. The money and the car would be very nice, he had to admit, but what was bothering him was the competitor's reputation for being a 'hire and fire' outfit. What's more, he'd been instrumental over the last few years in taking a lot of business from them and there were rumours flying round the trade that they were suffering from cashflow problems. However, whilst exercising his mind with these misgivings, Frank received another phone call from the competitor – this time to improve the offer by including a bonus arrangement for any new business he brought in.

We all have our price, or so we're told, but succumbing to enticement (accepting the offer you can't refuse) is one of the most common reasons why people make bad moves.

Enticement can come in many forms – pay, cars, perks and, these days, big up-front lump sum payments or 'golden hellos'. Going back to Frank's case study, the company making the approach is clearly quite desperate to get him on board (presumably to help them get back the business they have lost). Yet there are warning bells sounding already in Frank's head that their commitment to him may not be long-term. Indeed, all the signs are there that Frank will be shown the door as soon as he's been bled dry of his contacts.

Key point

A job with a fat cat salary and a fancy car won't do you much good if it only lasts six months. This is why you need to be very careful if you feel you are being made an offer you can't refuse – it could mean that the employer you're in negotiation with is in dire straits and knows no other way of getting you to take the job. For this reason, learn to take note of any warning bells that are ringing – all offers are refusable. Don't be afraid to say 'no'.

Using assertiveness with head-hunters

If you've made a good job of your career management, you should at some stage become the target for an approach. Approaches can come:

- direct from employers (as in Frank's case);
- from professional search consultants, or head-hunters.

Key point

If you are approached by head-hunters, see this as a golden opportunity to make major steps forward with your career. It's now down to you and your assertiveness skills.

Receiving an approach

As Frank found, approaches can tend to come at you:

- out of the blue;
- irrespective of whether you're on the job market or not.

For this reason, approaches can take you by surprise and at a time when you've not thought your ideas out fully. For example, the phone rings one evening while you're watching television and a voice at the other end of the line is asking if you'd be interested in a position with their company or not. How do you respond?

Like Frank, you may find you don't know quite what to say, in which case a convenient way to buy time is to plead it's difficult to talk just at the moment and say you'll call back. What you need to do now is prepare yourself to enter into a dialogue with an *aim*. The aim in this case is to move the dialogue forward, and the answer you need to give has to convey:

- confidence in your ability ('I'm sure I can do the job');
- the impression that, although you are happy with your present position, you would never rule out any move that would be advantageous to your career, i.e. you're open to offers.

Warning

Don't let the suddenness with which an approach is made knock you off balance. In particular, don't shut down an approach before it gets off the ground by negative, off-the-cuff comments that aren't properly thought out.

Setting out your stall

What kind of offer is it going to take to move you from Company A to Company B? Sooner or later this question is going to come up, so you need to be ready for it. A big mistake at this point is to talk yourself down by citing figures and benefits packages that are too low. Why?

- Most companies enter into an approach with very flexible ideas on pay and perks and are prepared to negotiate. In any negotiation it's easier to come down than it is to talk your way back up.

- With a top job, you could create the impression that you're lacking in personal ambition (something that would be seen as a bad point).
- You might be offered the job but on a package that doesn't interest you.

Key point

Being the target of an approach usually means one of the following:

- You've got talents, skills and experience that the people behind the approach are keen to acquire.
- You can bring knowledge that has some commercial advantage to them.
- The people behind the approach feel comfortable with you, either because they know you or because they have got good reports on you.

In all of these situations you have quite considerable bargaining power and, providing you use it, you can strike good deals with employers who single you out for an approach. The key points to remember are:

- Never sell yourself short.
- Put a proper (high) value on your worth.
- Negotiate if necessary, but don't talk yourself down.

Remember, too, the leverage is on your side. If the approach fails, you simply go back to what you're doing whereas the employer will be back where he/she started, and possibly facing a big bill if professional head-hunters have been used to make the approach to you (a big bill with nothing to show).

Questions and answers

Assertiveness and the unemployed

Q *Assertiveness with job applications sounds all well and good but, in my case, I've been unemployed for the last seven months and, for this reason, I would be happy to take any job that comes along, just to get my finances back on track. Am I right therefore in thinking this isn't for me?*

A Yes you are right. It would be silly to start laying down stipulations about what you expect from your next job when there are financial pressures bearing down on you. What you need to do first is take away the pressures by getting a job, even though it may not be one that is totally to your liking. You can then use your assertiveness to shop round for a better job – doing it, of course, from a position of greater strength.

Dangers of asking for too much

Q *With head-hunters, despite what you say about selling yourself short, isn't there a danger of asking for too much and effectively putting an end to the approach?*

A Though we understand what you're saying, you need to consider that head-hunters move in a world of big commissions where sentiments such as 'being too greedy' or 'going over the top' have little or no meaning. If your aspirations are too high then the head-hunter will tell you rather than abort the approach out of shock. The head-hunter will also be able to advise you on how far the people behind the approach are prepared to negotiate. In these situations it's always best to play hard to get. This is how you will stretch employers into making their best offer.

Summary

Assertiveness with a job application means controlling the direction it goes in and not leaving it to some mystical process of chance. The advantage to you is the far greater likelihood of you ending up with a job that you want.

In this chapter we have seen:

- how it pays to have clearly thought-out ideas on where you want your job moves to take you *in advance* of putting in any applications;
- how it's important to communicate your aspirations so that everyone knows where you're coming from and what you're seeking to achieve (the mismatches are thrown out automatically and the time-wasting and discouragement are avoided);
- how assertiveness correctly exploited in job interviews helps ensure that the right message gets across;

- the importance of an assertive approach when networking for jobs (keeping in control);
- the strength of your bargaining power when you've been offered a job and how, with the help of assertiveness, you can renegotiate any terms on offer that aren't to your liking;
- how assertiveness includes feeling able to decline offers that don't come up to scratch – particularly where you are being offered inducements to say yes (enticements);
- how assertiveness can help you to make the most of being on the receiving end of an approach.

08 assertiveness in professional networking

In this chapter you will learn:

- **how assertiveness will help you build up a circle of useful contacts**
- **how to make professional networks work for you**
- **the importance of staying in control**

Professional networking is the business of using your contacts to advance your career in the direction you want it to go. It is a very powerful tool and we are going to devote this final chapter of the book to exploring:

- the part played by assertiveness in developing effective networks;
- how assertiveness will help you to get your networks to perform.

Building professional networks

For many of us, the word 'networking' is a complete turn-off. We associate it with the kind of social functions where people hand out business cards and see how many phone numbers of potentially useful contacts they can collect. We feel we don't fit into this world. As a consequence, we feel networking isn't for us. We exclude ourselves.

Networks are organic

For those of you who find the idea of professional networking difficult to grasp, the first point to make is that everyone has a network whether they like the idea or not, and it has nothing to do with how many dinner parties they go to or how good they are at mixing. In fact, it could be said that a professional network is an almost unavoidable by-product of being in a career. As an example, the average network of someone working in the world of business would consist of the following:

- people you meet in your education;
- people who go into similar fields of work as you;
- your bosses, peers, subordinates – people who work in the same organization;
- people you worked with in previous jobs – people you have kept in touch with;
- external contacts – people you have business dealings with, such as customers and suppliers;
- professional contacts – people you meet through institutions you belong to or trade organizations.

Notepad

Networks are organic. They need no artificial growth stimulants.

Assertiveness and networks

Rather than spend your time worrying about the challenge of impressing your credentials on an ever-increasing number of people, the focus of your attention at the start would be better placed on:

- examining who you are networking with currently;
- whether they come up to standard.

The following case study will help to illustrate what you are trying to achieve by carrying out this exercise:

Case study 21: Marie and Nigel

Marie works for a firm of management consultants where she specializes in financial reporting procedures. She is 28, doing well and in line for promotion.

One evening Marie gets a phone call from Nigel who she worked with in a previous job. Nigel is down on his luck. He has been made redundant from the company he joined six months ago and he has been unemployed for the last four weeks. The purpose of Nigel's call is to ask Marie if she can help by putting in a word for him with her firm.

After finishing the conversation with Nigel and saying she'll see what she can do, Marie soon finds she is starting to have misgivings. Nigel's work ethic is notoriously poor to the point where lack of commitment and failure to meet deadlines have been the reasons why so many employers have decided to part company with him. Indeed Marie is highly suspicious that he may have lost his last job due to his personal failings rather than because of redundancy. What is bothering her now, of course, is that she will be putting her own reputation on the line if she recommends Nigel to her seniors. They may offer him a job on the strength of her recommendation – then how will she be placed if Nigel stays true to form and lapses back into his bad old ways? He will be exited pretty quickly, she is sure of that, but some of the mud is bound to stick on her in the process, and this could jeopardize her promotion. No, Marie decides, she is going to have to tell Nigel she can't help. She realizes she is going to find it difficult. She has been on the receiving end of a number of favours from Nigel in the past and she feels bad about putting her own considerations first.

Full marks to Marie for not giving in to the pangs of conscience she is experiencing as she turns her back on Nigel in his moment of need. Full marks to her for appreciating that:

- she wouldn't escape unscathed if Nigel became a problem to the seniors in her firm;
- some of the blame for taking him on would almost certainly attach to her.

Whether this would interfere with Marie's promotion or not is another matter, but it wouldn't be helpful to her, that's for certain.

Two-way traffic

What the case study of Marie and Nigel demonstrates is a fundamental principle of networking practice – it's two-way traffic. You network someone; someone networks you back. Someone does you a favour; sooner or later they will be expecting a favour in return. The idea, of course, is that this mutual back-scratching works to everyone's advantage, but the idea falls down if you happen to be networking with someone you're not happy to extend favours to. You don't feel you can trust them with confidential information or, like Marie, you don't feel comfortable about recommending them for a job because there's a chance they could let you down.

Key point

Don't fight shy when it comes to disengaging from people who don't measure up. Be assertive. Decide who you want in your network and who you don't. Keep the selection standards high.

Applying selectivity to networks

Whilst telling you to be firm and not to fudge when it comes to being choosy with the people you include in your circle of contacts, it doesn't help you when you're faced with the kind of situation that Marie found herself in. How do you tell someone you can't help them when you've been happy to take favours from them in the past? How do you distance yourself from someone who you've known a long time?

The answer is to be found in the two-way nature of networking relationships and the fact that the relationship between you and one of your contacts will have a natural tendency to wither and die if the traffic becomes all one way. What this means in practice is that if you don't solicit good turns from someone, then they will find it harder to call in the favours and solicit good turns back. In Marie's case she needs to:

- stick to her decision to say that she can't help;
- not ask Nigel for any more favours.

Making networks perform

Having looked at being assertive when it comes to shedding people from your network who no longer come up to standard, let's turn our attention next to getting networks to perform in the way that you want them to perform.

What's in it for you?

Having an effective professional network has many benefits in terms of advancing your career. Here are a few examples:

- **Applying for jobs:** Use your network to open doors for you and pull strings; likewise use your network to find out more about prospective employers.
- **Keeping in touch with the outside world:** Use your network as a source of information on what the market has to offer people with your talents; find out how your salary matches up; find out whether your skills are up-to-date and in line with what the market wants (your employability).
- **Changing careers:** Use your network to access opportunities to break into new fields.
- **Getting head-hunted:** Use your network as the infrastructure for receiving approaches; have contacts with the connections to put the right words in the right ears.
- **Getting business:** Tap into contacts for introductions.
- **Where you work for yourself:** Use your network to source work; the same goes for people who rely on contracts or short-term assignments.
- **Going into business:** Team up with the right people and use your network for this purpose.

Your network is there to be used

Given that everyone in a career has got a network and that networking is such a powerful tool, it's surprising how many people don't use it, or only use it in moments of desperation (for example, when they've just been handed their redundancy notice).

A good way to think about a network is that it's like a piece of precision machinery. If you use it and keep it in good running order it performs beautifully. Conversely, if you only switch it on occasionally, you'll find the moving parts don't function very well, and sometimes it doesn't start!

The most common reason for a network not performing very well is sheer neglect. A network is not something you pick up when you have a need and then put down when the need is no longer there. If you proceed in this way you will find you are constantly in the awkward position of having to make cold starts. The name of a contact you used to have will slip your memory, or the person will have moved on. The point is this: networks don't respond to stop–start treatment. The more you use them, the better they perform.

Notepad

This is the message in reverse to the point we made earlier about the way to shed people from your network who don't come up to scratch. Don't ring them and they won't ring you.

Overcome barriers to networking

Why do some people hold back when it comes to asking one of their contacts to do them a favour or pull a few strings? What makes them reluctant about picking up the phone? A few years ago we put these questions to a group of unemployed job-seekers. From those who had significantly failed to use networking to source opportunities, the answer we most frequently got back was that they felt uncomfortable about phoning up ex-colleagues and asking for help. Whether this was because they feared rejection, or whether it was because they felt it was a bit of a cheek, wasn't very clear. However, what we clearly had here was an assertiveness issue. People didn't attach sufficient importance to themselves to feel that they warranted favours and, in this case, it was proving to be a major impediment to them in getting back into paid employment.

As we said earlier, the key point to understand about networking is that the traffic is two-way. If you're asking someone to help you to find a job, the subtext to what you're saying is, 'I'll return the favour some day.' The benefits to networking are mutual. The other party stands to gain as much as you do.

What if someone gives you the cold shoulder and says they can't help? Award them a black mark. Put them on the list for deselection as far as membership of your network is concerned.

Why should anyone want to network with you?

Those with low self-esteem frequently ask themselves this one. The answer is that people have got to feel they are going to gain something from networking with you, and the best way to demonstrate this is by being receptive to their approaches. You must therefore be helpful and welcoming at all times. Conversely, what you must never do is put up the shutters to anyone who networks with you either because you're too busy or because what they're asking you to do seems like a tall order.

Key point

Always have time for your contacts. Let them see that nothing is too much trouble. Let them see at the same time that being on your network confers a special privilege on them and networking with you is worth it.

Controlling the messages

Control is a key networking word and, to see why, we need to refer back to the case study of Seb and Anthony in the last chapter (case study 17).

Complete messages

The lesson in the case study was to be assertive and to tell people who you're on networking terms with exactly what you want them to do for you. In particular, any messages you feed out need to be *complete* messages so that the person on the receiving end knows exactly where you are coming from and what you are seeking to achieve. In Seb's case, griping into his beer about pay sent Anthony off with half the message. He read into Seb's remarks that his only concern was over money and he acted on this information by getting him the interview with Ray.

Control the messages

Was Anthony to blame for taking too much on himself and not checking with Seb before speaking to Ray? Perhaps, but what the case study also illustrates is that people who you network with will do their best to help you – not least because you have probably done your best to help them in the past.

Questions and answers

Working rooms

Q *You make no mention of going to networking groups, working rooms or any of the other tips that books on networking tend to give. Why is this?*

A One of our central messages about networking is that it's for everyone and, let's face it, not everyone would feel comfortable about doing the kind of things you describe. Fine, if you are but, if you're not, then it's important not to feel excluded.

Networking is for social climbers and extroverts

Q *I associate networking with social climbers and extrovert personality types. Since I don't fit into either category, is it for me?*

A As we said in the answer to the last question, networking is for everyone, and everyone does it – including you, though you may not realize it. As for social climbers and extrovert personality types, they are often not the best when it comes to networking. Typically they tend to put their effort into networking with more and more people so that they end up with a network that is either too big, they don't use, or is out of control.

Getting Seb out of his dilemma

Q *It's clear that Seb in case study 17 has got himself into a bit of a mess, but what would you do in his shoes?*

A Concern for Anthony is important, but it can't be allowed to get in the way of such an important decision as whether to accept a job offer or not. In other words, this is a decision he needs to make for the right reasons – what the job offers and how far it goes towards moving him in the direction he wants to go in. The difficulty arises if Seb turns the offer down. Ray might well feel slighted or that his time has been wasted, and some of his annoyance could come Anthony's way. What should Seb do? Perhaps before phoning Ray to tell him his decision Seb should speak to Anthony first. That way Anthony would at least be prepared for the flak and it would give him the option of speaking to Ray and explaining his position. What Seb could find, of course, is that Anthony won't be quite so enthusiastic to help him in the future.

Summary

Networking is one of the most powerful tools at the disposal of people in careers, and effort put into it is usually effort that pays off hands down. In this chapter we have looked at how an assertive approach to networking helps when it comes to:

- combing out people who shouldn't be in your network (dictating the standards);
- overcoming any resistance to using your network (don't hold back on calling in the favours);
- sending out clear messages (everyone knows what's expected of them).

Remember too that a good, effective network is part of adding value to yourself. If you can pull strings, access knowledge and information then people will look up to you and take you seriously.

Bargaining power

Do add to your value at every opportunity.
Don't try to be assertive when you don't have the clout to carry it through.

Clarity

Do keep the messages sharp and concise.
Don't confuse the people you are seeking to convince.

Consensus

Do search out the common ground.
Don't get into conflict.

Delivery

Do keep the messages positive.
Don't fog the issues with grumbles and grouses.

Empowerment

Do know what you're talking about.
Don't be assertive unless you're sure you're right.

Engagement

Do plan for the dialogue.
Don't be left floundering because your arguments have run out of steam.

Finances

Do stay in control.
Don't let your life be taken over by money troubles.

Image

Do seek to inspire confidence.
Don't be let down by your personal appearance.

Life skills

Do keep people on your side.
Don't put their backs up.

Preparation

Do think through what you're going to say.
Don't proceed with half-baked arguments.

Priorities

Do pick issues that are important to you.
Don't use assertiveness when the outcomes don't matter.

Reality

Do face up to it when assertiveness isn't working.
Don't battle on with lost causes.

Relationships

Do keep your distance from people who undermine you.
Don't expose yourself to negative influences.

Responsibility

Do take charge of the messages.
Don't blame others when the messages fail to come across.

Style

Do what you're comfortable with.
Don't do anything that doesn't come naturally.

Team spirit

Do listen to what other people are saying.
Don't shut your ears to their ideas.

Work

Do give your best to every day.
Don't broadcast your flaws.

Building your own word power

Expanding your vocabulary will help you to:

- express your ideas and opinions more fluently;
- instil confidence in others;
- be more assertive and creative with your arguments.

Making it a habit to read with a dictionary and to write down any new words you come across together with their meaning will give you a foundation for developing your flair with language and improving your communication skills. Aim to build up a list of, say, a thousand words and test yourself randomly on them from time to time. Better still, build up a word list with a friend or partner and have competitions with one another.

Books

Interest in assertiveness has soared in recent years and a search of any major bookseller's website will reveal a large number of titles. Here is just a small selection:

Ken and Kate Back, *Assertiveness at Work*, 1999, McGraw Hill

Sue Bishop, *Develop your Assertiveness*, 2000, Kogan Page

Madelyn Burley-Allen, *Managing Assertively: How to improve your people skills*, 1995, John Wiley

Max A. Eggert, *The Assertiveness Pocket Book*, 1997, Management Pocket Books

Jan Ferguson, *Perfect Assertiveness,* 2003, Random House

Terry Gillen, *Assertiveness*, 1998, CIPD

Dena Michelli, *Assertiveness in a Week*, 2002, Hodder & Stoughton, Chartered Management Institute

Paddy O'Brien, *Assertiveness – A Working Guide*, 1990, Nicholas Brearley

In addition, readers who would like to develop their understanding of silent bargaining power as a tool of career management may be interested in trying two of our other books in the Teach Yourself series:

Managing You Own Career, 2003

Getting a Pay Rise, 2000

Courses

Courses in assertiveness are offered by a large number of training institutions. To find out what's available near to you keep your eyes on the local press and/or tap into the websites of colleges and adult learning centres in your area. Courses run by well-known management development organizations tend to be expensive and could possibly be out of your reach. Some employers are happy to fund the cost of attending courses particularly where they see benefits in terms of improved job performance.

Useful websites

www.reed.co.uk/training
www.courses.uk.com
www.nec.ac.uk
www.essex.ac.uk
www.bradford.ac.uk
www.st-andrews.ac.uk

index

teach yourself

managing your own career

pat scudamore and hilton catt

- Do you feel that you're in an employment rut?
- Do you need to decide whether to stay put or make a move?
- Are you considering working for yourself?

Managing Your Own Career deals with modern career situations in which employees need to take their own decisions and don't look to employers to provide them with the answers. It allows you to stay in control and manage both the ups and downs of your career so you can tailor your work to suit your individual needs.

Pat Scudamore and **Hilton Catt** have worked in all areas of human resources and business training. They now run the Scudamore Catt Partnership, a successful human resources management and training business, and are the authors of numerous books on career management.

teach yourself

time management

polly bird

- Do you need to maximize your time?
- Do you want to minimize your clutter and chaos at work?
- Do your days need restructuring?

Time Management shows you how to declutter your life by recording, monitoring and improving your use of time – and helps you to cut down on stress, achieve your goals, improve your performance at work and free up more time for your personal needs. It contains practical advice on prioritizing, planning your time, reducing paperwork, handling phone calls, delegating, training staff… and learning to say 'no'!

Polly Bird is a professional writer of business and training books.

teach yourself

negotiating

phil baguley

- Are you new to negotiating?
- Do you want to cover the basics then progress fast?
- Do you need to brush up your skills?

Negotiating is an important book for all professionals. Negotiating is increasingly a part of business life at all levels and in all organizations. This book will help you to develop and improve your skills and increase your negotiating strike-rate, with real-life case studies and checklists.

Phil Baguley is a business writer and lecturer. He has held senior management roles in multinational corporations and worked as a management consultant throughout Europe.

teach yourself

performance management

phil baguley

- Are you in business or setting up your own company?
- Do you want to learn performance management techniques?
- Do you need to improve your performance management skills?

Performance Management will provide the information, skills and knowledge that you need to begin and sustain the process of successful performance management. It will give you a clear understanding of the what, how, why and when of successful performance management, access to a tool-kit of techniques to enhance your performance management ability and a firm foundation of knowledge.

Phil Baguley is a business writer and lecturer. He has held senior management roles in multinational corporations and worked as a management consultant throughout Europe.

teach yourself

recruitment

edward peppitt

- Are you recruiting for the first time?
- Do you need to learn interviewing and recruitment skills quickly?
- Do you need guidance in making the right choice?

Recruitment is a vital reference source for every manager who has responsibility for recruiting staff. It guides the busy manager through the minefield of recruitment, including planning, recruitment methods, short listing, interview techniques, selecting the ideal candidate and ensuring success for the chosen candidate. Checklists and tips illustrate each topic, while case studies help to apply the theories in everyday situations.

Edward Peppitt is a business and publishing consultant, and author of *The Investors in People Toolbox*.

teach yourself

winning at job interviews

igor popovich

- Are you new to the job market?
- Are you contemplating a return to work?
- Do you want to boost your confidence at interviews?

Winning at Job Interviews shows you how to be the best applicant for the job you want. Its clear, step-by-step format covers both basic and advanced strategies for winning in the job market, with sample questions and model answers to help you recognize your strengths and weaknesses, evaluate interview situations and deal with difficult questions.

Igor S. Popovich is the director of a career-help consultancy which offers training courses on interviewing, job hunting and career management.